DAILY DEVOTIONS WITH UCHIMURA KANZO

MORIYUKI ABUKUMA (EDITOR)

DAILY DEVOTIONS WITH UCHIMURA KANZO

MORIYUKI ABUKUMA (EDITOR)

Daily Devotions with Uchimura Kanzo

Moriyuki Abukuma (Editor)

Published by Foundation University Press

Verrijn Stuartweg 31, Diemen 1112 AW, The Netherlands

www.foundationuniversitypress.com

This book or parts thereof may not be reproduced in any form, stored in a retrieval system or transmitted in any form by any means-electronic, mechanical, photocopy, recording or otherwise-without prior written permission of the publisher, except as provided by the European Copyright Law and United States of America Copyright Law.

ISBN: 978-94-90179-05-2

Copyright © 2010 by Foundation University Press

Unless otherwise noted, all Scripture quotations are from the Holy Bible, American King James Version.
Copyright © 1999.

Credits

Daily Devotions With Uchimura Kanzo consists of *Ichinichi Issho* edited by Hanzo Azegami (153 days), *Zoku Ichinichi Issho* edited by Taizo Yamamoto (157 days), and Uchimura's English works, *Alone with God* (57 days) and *The Japan Christian Intelligencer* (10 days). The Translation of "Ichinichi Issho" and "Zoku Ichinichi Issho" is based on Itojiro Morimoto's work (Published by Nenrin, an old People's Home, Sakai, Japan, 1992) for 249 days. The translation of "Non-church" and 24th Feburary is taken from *Sources of Japanese Tradition* (Tsunoda *et al.*, 1973).

Foreword

Uchimura Kanzo (1861–1930) is one of the most prominent Japanese Christian thinkers, the world has ever known. He was born in a Samurai family during the ending years of the Tokugawa period in 1861. Later, during the Meiji Period, Japan's modernization era, he studies at the Sapporo Agricultural School, the current Hokkaido University. During his years at agricultural school from 1878–81, he gave his life to Jesus Christ.

After his conversion experience and his intense studies of the Holy Scriptures, Uchimura Kanzo gradually was confronted with a very difficult reality: the Western missionaries did not only brought Christianity to Japan, but also their own cultures in the name of Christianity. He saw that Christianity brought by Westerners carried Western cultural agenda with it. This itself was not the major problem to Uchimura Kanzo, what bothered him the most was in fact the arrogance and pride in some Western missionaries. Uchimura often mentioned that not one single nation has even been saved entirely by foreign missionaries. He mentioned that on contrary, missionaries destroyed countries instead of building them. From Mexico's Montezuma and Peruvian Incan empires, Christianity's course has been absorption, destruction, and, in some cases even annihilation. Western Christendom, he mentioned kills non-Christian countries by introducing rum and whisky, and tobacco; by its many foul diseases.

Uchimura Kanzo said that a Roman Catholicism is only good for the Roman culture, and Anglican Christianity emerged from English culture, and a Lutheran emerged from Germany and German culture. Why then not have to have a Japanese Christianity that is fully compatible to both Japan and Jesus. And I would say we have European Christianity in all its variations, why not African Christianity with all its colorful variations? Or Asian or Indian? Therefore Uchimura Kanzo became a promoter of independent church, free from control and financial bondage to the headquarters that are run by those outside Japan.

Later Uchimura Kanzo's ideas were crystallized into a movement called "Non-Church" movement, or *Mukyukai*. Uchimura Kanzo did not believe in the organized Church. Uchimura Kanzo was often hated by the Japanese, because of his love for Jesus. He was misunderstood the Christians, because of his passion for Japan. Uchimura said: "I love two Js and no third; one is Jesus, and the other is Japan. I do not know which I love more, Jesus or Japan. I am hated by my countrymen for Jesus' sake as foreign belief, and I am disliked by foreign missionaries for Japan's sake as national and narrow. Even if I lose all my friends, I cannot lose Jesus and Japan... Jesus and Japan; my faith is not a circle with one center; it is an ellipse with two centers. My heart and mind revolve around the two dear names. And I know that one strengthens the other; Jesus strengthens and purifies my love for Japan; and Japan clarifies and objectives my love for Jesus. Were it not for the two, I would become a mere dreamer, a fanatic, an amorphous universal man." After more than a century, the ideas of Uchimura Kanzo are living again. It is interesting to know that the idea of the Non-Church movement fits in our current times of history.

Further, Uchimura Kanzo was a promoter of nature. He saw the beauty of nature as part of Gods creation, and he urged the need of caring for the nature. Often nature played an important role in Uchimura's expression of faith both in his theological writings and in his poetry. The love for nature was of course not the case with his contemporary Western Christianity, which was promoting capitalism and free market economy that lead eventually to the catastrophic climate change and erosion of the earth.

Uchimura Kanzo influenced many Japanese political figures as well as well known writers, among them the writers Masamune Hakucho, Mushanokoji Saneatsu, and Arimisha Takeo, who in 1910 founded the influential *Shirakaba* "White Birch", a journal that served as a vehicle for their humanitarian ideals.

Uchimura Kanzo is only one example of many other Japanese theologians and Christians of his time. Toyohiko Kagawa (1888–1960), for example. If the Western Christians would have offered their listening ears to these great men, the face of Christianity was very different than what it is today, especially in Japan.

This book is published with the permission of Dr. Moriyuki Abukuma, to whom I am deeply grateful. This book is a diary with the beautiful, insightful and inspirational words of Uchimura Kanzo. This is a 365 days journey with Uchimura Kanzo.

In Solidarity with Uchimura Kanzo,

Dr. Samuel Lee
Foundation University, The Netherlands
President

Uchimura's Self-introduction

My name is Uchimura Kanzo. A Japanese, a son of samurai, an independent Christian; in profession, a book writer, a magazine-editor, a teacher in the Christian Bible. Was born in Tokyo, on the 23rd of March, 1861, according to the Gregorian calendar, eight years after Commodore Perry anchored in the Bay of Yedo. Began to study English at the age of 14; but never mastered it. Sent to the Foreign Language School, to prepare for the Kaiseigakko, now the Tokyo Imperial University but was induced to enter the Sapporo Agricultural College, then started by the Colonial Departments under the presidency of William. S. Clark, Ph.D., LL.D. of Amherst, Mass., U.S.A. Graduated from that college in 1881. Served in the Agricultural Department for 3 years. Went to America in 1884, mainly to learn methods of practical philanthropy. Came under the guidance of Isaac N. Kerlin, M. D. the superintendent of the Pennsylvania Institute for Feeble-minded Children, at Elwyn, Delaware County of that state. While there, met James B. Richards, a veteran teacher of the mental defective. Was introduced to President Julius H. Seelye of Amherst College, Mass. by Mr. Joseph H. Nijima. Joined the junior year of the class of 1887, and stayed there until graduation. The great president opened my eyes to the evangelical truth in Christianity. He is my father in faith. For forty years, since then, I preached the faith taught me by that venerable teacher. On my return to Japan in 1888, I made several attempts to put my educational ideas to practice, but always failed. Missionaries nicknamed me a "school-breaker," because wherever I taught, troubles arose, and schools were put in jeopardy. My fortunes in Government schools were worse. My refusal to bow to the Imperial Rescript on Education, not only deprived me of my situation in the Dai Ichi Kotogakko, but sent me out into Japanese society as a vagabond, wherein for some 20 years, I had not a place where to lay my head on. But I was more successful in book writing and journalism. During the last 30 years I wrote about 30 books, which though not "good-sellers," were some of them, good survivors, and are still read after the expiration of the copy-right. I joined the editorial staff of the *Yorodzu Choho* in 1895, and there met the managing editor of this magazine, and I have kept up friendship with him till this time. After three years, I started my own paper, the *Tokyo Independent,* which was succeeded by the *Biblical Studies* in 1900, which is continued to this day. Then I did much of preaching, lecturing, and Bible-expositions, the most notable of which was a large Bible-class in the Hygienic Hall, in front of the Home Department, not far from the Imperial Castle. I started the class in 1918, till it was interrupted by the earthquake ravage five years afterward; but now resumed in my own precinct, though on somewhat smaller scale. I am a free-lance in my religious standing; join no church, never "licensed" to preach by any ecclesiastical authority; entirely independent. My two books which I wrote in English were translated into several European languages, enabling me to find many friends in the continental Europe. The books failed in America; Englishmen never liked them. I pass for a rabid *yaso* (follower of Jesus) among my countrymen, and a heretic and dangerous man among missionaries and their converts in this country. Still I seem to have not a few friends in this wide world; for my magazine, — the Bible-magazine' written in my own language, — has quite a large circulation, and my books translated into German are still being read in Europe. I on my own part, take, or try to take, all honest, sincere men and women, as my friends and allies; and though some of them may dislike me, that is no reason why I should dislike them in return. I am a Japanese by birth, and a Christian in faith; and my Christianity made me a "Buerger der Welt," a world-citizen, a brother to humanity. With the managing editor, I am an advocate of peace. Both of us are haters of war. We take comparatively little interest in politics. But we love God, the world, the soul. With this self-introduction, may I find favor with the readers in the wide, wide world!

March, 1926.

Non-Church

"Non-church" is the church for those who have no church. It is the home for those who have no home, the orphanage for the orphan in spirit....

The true form of the church is non-church. There is no organized church in heaven. John says, "I saw no temple (church) within the city (heaven)" (Revelation 21: 22). Bishops, deacons, preachers, and teachers exist only here on earth. In heaven, there is neither baptism nor communion; neither teachers nor students....

Naturally, however, as long as we remain on this earth, we need churches. Some people will join churches constructed by the hands of humans; there they will praise God, and there they will hear his word. Some churches will be made of stone, others of brick, and still others of wood. But not all of us need churches of this sort. That there are many Christians who do not belong to organized Christianity is similar to the fact that there are many homeless children. But even those of us who do not belong to organized Christianity need some sort of church while we exist on this earth. Where is our church and what is it like?

[*Uchimura Kanzo Zenshu,* Tokyo: Iwanami Shoten, 1963, vol. IX, pp. 210–213]. Tsunoda *et al., Sources of Japanese Tradition,* New York: Columbia Univ. Press, 1958, pp. 854–5.

01 January

In the beginning God created the heaven and the earth.

Genesis 1: 1

Creation of Universe

Christian concept of the universe and human life centers around this short verse. The universe, vast and unfathomable, is a creation of God. Hence, its change and movement should be at His will. The universe is my Father's garden, wherein I live with nothing to fear. Let me leave this country for another; there is He. Let me leave the earth for Jupiter or Mercury; there He surely is. God abides in the Orion and the Pleiades. Even in another universe, apart from this, there my Father should be as well. With God, the universe represents a paradise for me as His child,. There, let me praise His wonderful work singing His glory, and let me die with a sure hope that His hands would receive me to lead me into a new world and a new Jerusalem, to praise His Holy Name eternally.

02 January

Do you not know that you are a temple of God, and that the Spirit of God dwells in you? If anyone defiles the temple of God, God shall destroy him. For the temple of God is holy, which you are.

1 Corinthians 3: 16-17

Creation of Human

"God created human in his own image" (*Genesis 1: 27*). If the universe is the substance of God, is human body made of the universe? Then, if human is fashioned after the universe, does human externally too represent God's image? This is not to humanize God, but to elevate human standards to the height of God. "Your body is the temple of the Holy Spirit in you, which you have of God, and you are not your own" (*1 Corinthians 6: 19*). Human looks upon one's body with contempt, as mere flesh of animal, and does not know how precious and holy it is. When one defiles one's body, one defiles God's holy image. Are not our bodies the holy temple, made after His supreme image? Holy Jehovah, Lord of Hosts.

03   January

First Dream

  Dew of grace dropped on the top of Mt. Fuji, trickled down to its foot and flowed over into two streams, one eastward and the other westward.
The one crossed the sea, washed the Mt. Paektu, soaked the Kunluns, watered the foot of the Tien Shan and the Himalayas, and ended in the wilderness of Judea.
The other crossed the Pacific Ocean, quenched the fire of gold-worship at the foot of the Rockies, purified the Holy of Holies on the banks of the Mississippi and the Hudson, and submerged into the Atlantic Ocean.
Seeing it, peaks of the Alps sang with the morning star; the Sahara desert rejoiced to bloom like the saffron.
As water covering the ocean, the knowledge of Jehovah filled the whole earth, and the nations of this world became the Nation of Christ.
Awakened from this dream, I cried aloud solitarily, "Amen. Thus be it. You will be done on earth as in Heaven."

04   January

Now when Jesus was born in Bethlehem of Judea in the days of Herod the king, behold, there came wise men from the east to Jerusalem.

Matthew 2: 1

Birth of Savior

God opened the way of salvation for humans by sending His Son to be born in a manger where cattle and sheep feed, on a hill at Bethlehem, when legions in millions defended the borders while Caesar enjoyed a feast in the palace, proudly honoring his power and status. This is the usual way of great chances in the world. While the known world looks to an emperor and his armed forces for its realization, God sends a poor infant child to a stable to precede in a new era. Great chance is again clamored for. Let us now instead follow the wise men of the East and proceed direct to Bethlehem, rather than Rome, in search of our Savior.

05 January

Whatsoever is not of faith is sin.

Romans 14: 23

Cause of Evil

If goodness is to follow God, evil must be to leave God. Stealing, murder or adultery is sin not by itself, but by the result of leaving God. When I am condemned by law for murder, I am called upon not for violation of the homicide law itself but for leaving my God. I shall not commit a crime whatever tempted, or shall not even cherish an idea of sin, as long as God abides within me and I with Him. Defectiveness, contempt of others, desiring lust, arrogance, and neglecting my neighbors, all these result from leaving God. Consequently, I shall be able to do good only if I return to God. This indeed must be the only way to avoid sin.

06 January

Think not that I am come to send peace on earth; I came not to send peace, but a sword.

Matthew 10: 34

Way of Christian

Whoever comes to Christ in order to be Christianized will surely abandon Him. And, whoever comes to Christ for interest in thought or for a wider social intercourse will likewise abandon Him. Only those who are relived of their sins and come to Him for saving of their souls will remain with Him eternally. Anyone who approaches Christ aesthetically or philosophically or socially will depart from Him eventually. The would-be Christians must be aware of this reality.

07   January

We give thanks to God for you always, making mention of you in our prayers, remembering without ceasing your work of faith, and labor of love, and patience of hope in our Lord Jesus Christ, in the sight of God and our Father.

1 Thessalonians 1: 3

God, Resurrection and Christ

We believe in God's faithfulness. It is our hope to wait for the resurrection, the everlasting life and the approaching Nation of God. We follow the love of God, embodied by Christ who was crucified to die and rose again to eternal life. Faith, hope and love alone can conquer the world.

08   January

We have known and believed the love that God has in us. God is love, and the one who abides in love abides in God, and God in him or her.

1 John 4: 16

God is Love

Love is the greatest gift that God gives us. God may not necessarily give us power. He did not give it to Jesus. God did not grant upon His beloved Son the power to call down many of angels from heaven to destroy the enemies who ridiculed and mocked Him. He did not open His mouth, humbling Himself even amid torture. Like a lamb drawn for slaughtering, like a sheep dumb before the shearer, He did not open His mouth. But God gave Jesus of profound love, which led Him to cry from on the cross "Father, forgive them, for they do not know what they do" (*Luke 23: 34*). Jesus, on the cross, could not even avail Himself of the power to save Himself. But He proved to be the Son of God, weak and helpless, but lived with love alone.

09   January

I will lift up my eyes to the mountains.
Where shall my help come from?
My help comes from the LORD,
who made heaven and earth.
He will not allow your foot to be moved;
He who keeps you will not slumber.

Psalms 121: 1–3

Help Comes from God

What can I do with my feeble flesh? What can I do with my sinful society? I am disappointed with my flesh and society. But my help comes from Jehovah who created heaven and earth. He owns unfathomable power. And I open the door of my heart and fill it with His power. God helps my work with Holy Spirit and with miracles in heaven and earth. Thus, with Lord's help, I can alone stand against the whole world without any fear or anxiety.

10 January

The heart is deceitful above all things, and desperately wicked; who can know it? I the LORD search the heart, I try the reins, even to give to each person according to one's ways, according to the fruit of one's doings.

Jeremiah 17: 9–10

Renounce One's Self

"I abhor myself," said Job (*42: 6*). This is the sign of true repentance. Not abhorrence of the evil world, or of the fallen humanity, or of this and that person, but abhorrence of one's own self is the only condition of acceptance in the sight of God. Self is the seat of sin, and sin is selfishness. God abhors human's self; and a person must abhor one's self more than anything else, in order to be one with God. May I then abhor myself and repent in dust and ashes in the beginning of the year and at all times; so may God' pour grace upon me, and I dwell in Him who loved me and gave Himself for me.

11   January

O God, You do not require a rite of sacrifice; or else I would give it; You do not delight in burnt offering. True sacrifice to God is a broken spirit; a broken and a contrite heart, which You will not despise.

Psalms 51: 16–17

Broken Heart

We may offer our work and enterprise to God. But God ask us sacrifice of a heart more than our achievement. True sacrifice is to offer a broken heart, a childlike heart, or an innocent heart. We may be unable to offer the sacrifice of your enterprise, but we can offer our heart at any time. God may send us illness, perhaps, for this purpose. You may have wanted to serve Christ like Martha of Bethany and have found yourself "burdened about much serving" (*Luke 10: 40*). God may deprive of your working power to replace your heart with Mary's. "With emptied hands I cling to the Cross." Is this not the verse you used to pray? Your present inability to work must be meant to reveal a deeper meaning of serving.

12   January

LORD, I have loved the habitation of Your house, and the place where Your honor dwells.

Psalms 26: 8

God is All

We may lose our fortune, but shall not lose the belief in God. We may suffer sickness, but shall not be doubt the will of God. We may be despised by the people. But, do not forsake me, my God. Even we may passed over death joyously. But do not separate me from You, my God. You are all in all. Loss of God is loss of my whole being. Oh, dwell with me our Father, and I will suffice with it. My purpose of life is to find and live with my God, and nothing else.

13   January

We know that the law is spiritual, but I am carnal, sold under sin. For that which I do, I know not. For what I should, that I do not do; but what I should not, that I do.

Romans 7: 14–15

Conflicting Selves

Human should not commit sins, but he or she does. He or she has the duty and power to be pure, but cannot be pure. Though qualified to be an angel, he or she often degenerates into an animal. Human may mount to heaven as well as descend to hell. He or she may reach either boundless glory or bottomless misery. He or she stands in between the two extremes, the peak and the bottom. It is easy to descend ignoring the warning of conscience, but hard to mount following the will of climbing. What I should, I do not do; what I should not, I do. I have two selves always conflicting with each other. Truly, this life on earth must be a struggling life.

14   January

God was in Christ reconciling the world to Himself, not charging their sins to them, and putting the word of reconciliation in us. Then we are ambassadors on behalf of Christ, as God exhorting through us, we beseech you on behalf of Christ, be reconciled to God.

2 Corinthians 5: 19–20

Reconciliation to God

Salvation can come when one knows that sin means leaving God, and that righteousness is returning to God. Salvation is not just departing from sin and becoming a righteous person, since human does not have the power to do such commands. But salvation is God' redeeming of humankind to Himself, and human's returning to God. And Christ is the Mediator, enabling human to reconcile to God. That is, to reinstate humankind in its original being in relation with God.

15 January

Set your affection on things above, not on things on the earth. For you are dead, and your life is hid with Christ in God. When Christ, who is our life, shall appear, then you shall also appear with him in glory.

Colossians 3: 2–4

Concern Not of World

Christian's sole concern must not be about things on the earth, but in Heaven. This is because the Christian has already died in spirit and left the world, and Christian's life is hid in God with Christ. However, the Christian shall not be eternally hidden. When Christ shall come again in the glory of His resurrected body, we too shall appear in glory with Him. Therefore a Christian should not corrupt one's conscience by dwelling upon filthiness, jealousy, covetousness and other sins. The Bible teaches us to seek the Nation of Heaven and eternal life, and not be bothered by worldly things and not to waste life in baseness. These words aim us, by the way of a prophesy, to a pure life with high ideals.

16 January

Beloved, now we are children of God, and it does not yet appear what we shall be; but we know that, when He shall appear, we shall be like Him; for we shall see Him as He is.

1 John 3: 2

Completion of Salvation

A Christian lives in the midst of salvation. God began a wholesome work in him or her and will complete it at the day of Judgment. We need not lament our imperfection. We stay in the sinful world, where perfection, howsoever sought, is beyond our reach, as we are so corrupted both outside and inside. Thus, because of this state, "Ourselves also, which have the first fruits of the spirit, even we ourselves groan within ourselves, waiting for the adoption, to wit, the redemption of our body" (*Romans 8: 23*). And this revelation never fails; we will wait the time of the realization. The Second Advent of Christ means not only His second coming but also the completion of salvation of all Christians.

17   January

Woe is me, my mother, that You have borne me a man of strife and a man of contention to the whole earth. I have neither lent on usury, nor have men lent to me on usury; yet everyone curses me.

                              Jeremiah 15: 10

Woe is me

Once I sighed with Jeremiah, "Oh, woe is me. I was born a man of strife and a man of contention to the whole earth. Everyone curses me." But now I come to say with gratitude," Oh blessed am I, who could became one with God and enjoy His salvation, because people caused strife and contention with me and cursed me." People thrown me out, but God picked me up. People hated men, but God loved me. People shunned me, but God embraced me. Now I am convinced that, throughout my life, my utmost happiness has come from the contempt, hatred, affront and rejection by people.

18   January

Have you not known? Have you not heard, that the everlasting God, the LORD, the Creator of the ends of the earth, does not grow weak nor weary? There is no searching of His understanding. He gives power to the weary; He increases strength of the weak. Even the youths shall faint and be weary, and the young people shall utterly fall; but those who wait on the LORD shall renew their strength; they shall mount up with wings as eagles; they shall run, and not be weary; they shall walk and not faint.

Isaiah 40: 28–31

Dreamer

An ideal reaches its end when materialized. A person has reached one's last stage by the fruition of one's ideal. To be young forever, a person has to seek always an ideal that is yet to be realized. A youth is a dreamer. Without a dream, one is already dead being only interested in gain or loss. A person who is always poetic and dreaming, disregards gain or loss, and defies danger is a youth in the prime life. In contrast, a person of worthless, how older the age may be, is pursuing only the possible, living in the ordinary, being matter-of-fact and practical, being ever keen on gain or loss, and taking no forward step beyond the existing conditions.

19   January

Dearly beloved, let us cleanse ourselves from all filthiness of the flesh and spirit, perfecting holiness in the fear of God.

2 Corinthians 7: 1

Be Perfect

"Be therefore perfect, even as your Father which is in heaven is perfect" (*Matthew 5: 48*). This does not mean human can attain the absolute perfection of God but that human should be as perfect as human can be. A perfect horse does not mean the one that can speak and think like human, but one that functions perfectly as a horse. When therefore human is called sinful, this means human lacks perfectness as required of human. This is what Christianity teaches there is no righteous person among humans. God judges me, not because I did not let rain fall or less the sun shine, but because I despised humans instead of loving them, and manifested anger instead of forbearance.

20 January

Oh give thanks to the LORD; for He is good; _for His mercy endures forever.

Oh give thanks to the God of gods; _for His mercy endures forever.

Oh give thanks to the Lord of lords; _for His mercy endures forever.

To Him who alone does great wonders; _for His mercy endures forever.

Psalms 136: 1–4

Thanks of Heart

Thanksgiving makes an essential element of faith. True faith is with a heart of gratefulness. Or, where true faith exists there must be always overflowing thanks. "Faith is a thankful heart." Living, warm and heart-to-heart faith comes not from duties but from the depth of gratefulness. Such faith naturally yields the fruits of songs and good deeds.

21 January

I am the LORD, your Holy One, the creator of Israel, your King. Thus says the LORD, which makes a way in the sea, and a path in the mighty waters; Which brings forth the chariot and horse, the army and the power; they shall lie down together, they shall not rise; they are extinct, they are quenched as tow.

Isaiah 43: 15–17

What is Miracle

What is a miracle? A miracle is God's deed. That is, the deed done by God who created human and the universe. Human cannot perform a miracle unless specially endowed with God's gift. For, Human is not only formed by a part of the soil, but also lost one's innate power by corruption. We are initially created by the image of God, but fallen to the slave of nature. On the other hand, God is able to freely dictate the nature of His own creation. So wonder at all how God can quicken or delay the movement of the universe as if a watch maker sets the hands fast or slow freely.

22 January

I am found in Christ; not having my own righteousness, which is of the Law, but through the faith of Christ, the righteousness of God by faith, that I may know Him and the power of His resurrection and the fellowship of His sufferings, being made conformable to His death.

Philippians 3: 9–10

Know God's Will

Sickness is all right; I just want to know God's holy will. Poverty is all right; I just want to know God's holy will. Despising is all right; I just want to know God's holy will. Uttermost misery is my inability to know the Divine Will. I am not afraid of sickness, or poverty, or loneliness, but I do fear if I might be forsaken by God and be left ignorant of His Will. Oh God, grant the spiritual commission that will continue for ever between You and me, under whatsoever trials may fall upon me.

23   January

There are many plans in a human's heart; but the counsel of the LORD alone shall stand.

                                                        Proverbs 19: 21

Way to Vocation

Many a person says, "If I could know my mission, I would sacrifice everything for attaining it." Oh, human, you can already know your mission and find it easily. Concentrate all your energy on the work you are doing today. You will then be led to your mission unfailingly. Your mission does not come through heavenly voice or by your own thought. Your mission is revealed by the very work you are engaged in already. You are now on the way to reaching your mission. Why not do today's work with all your ability? Why do you delay in finding your mission by vain thinking? A proverb says, "Whatsoever your hands find to do, do it with your might." This is the way to find one's mission, and there is no other way. Plain and simple as it is, fulfilling today's work leads to the Nation of hope and the city of thanksgiving and joy.

24　January

I will pray the Father, and He shall give you another Comforter, who may abide with you for ever; He shall be the Spirit of truth; whom the world cannot receive, because it sees Him not, neither knows Him; but you know Him; for He dwells with you, and shall be in you. I will not leave you comfortless; I will come to you.

John 14: 16–18

Holy Spirit

We become a Christian not because we were baptized to join a church, not because we understood the Christian doctrine by our brain. But we become a Christian because we have received the "Holy One" as our friend. It is not that we discovered an ideal person in a historical record, but that we found a living and Holy Friend who accompanies us even at this moment. We indeed have obtained a great "Paraclete," namely, "one called alongside to help." Amid of the desolate world, we no longer feel loneliness but have now a great "Comforter" as our daily friend.

25   January

You are the light of the world. A city that is set on an hill cannot be hid. Neither do humans light a candle, and put it under a bushel, but on a candlestick; and it gives light to all that are in the house. Let your light so shine before humans, that they may see your good works, and glorify your Father which is in heaven.

Matthew 5: 14–16

Light of World

Disciples of Jesus are the light of the world. They are pioneers of civilization, developers of intelligence, suppliers of divine light. There is no doubt about this truth. So-called Christianity of the world may not be without superstition. So-called Christian churches have sometimes turned into the domes of stubborn ignorant. But no one, whosoever under any circumstances, can deny that, throughout the past 2,000 years of human history, the disciples of Jesus have acted as bearers of spiritual light. Jesus said "I am the light of the world" (*John 8: 20*). And His followers have lightened the world after Him. They cannot of course shed light of their own accord, but each will reflect His divine light according to the depth of one's faith,.

26   January

But what am I?
An infant crying in the night;
An infant crying for the light,
And with no language but a cry.

Tennyson, Alfred "Stanza 5"

Eternal Soul and Other World

The poet Tennyson paid his greatest attention to the problems of the eternity of the soul and of the existence of the other world. The late Gladstone also gave his lifelong thoughts to the same subjects and at his last moments, and wrote his commentary upon Butler's "Analogy of religion," leaving the outcome of his rich observation and deep thoughts to the world. Whether a states-person, literary person, business person, or factory worker, it is essential for any person to embrace an goal above and beyond this world, so that his character may be heightened, his conscience purified and he may get rid of the worry of being stained by secular atmosphere.

27 January

Faithful is He that calls you, who also will do it.

1 Thessalonians 5: 24

God is Faithful

God is faithful. Oh blessed words. He changes not. Whatever He plans He accomplishes. He, not our wills or resolutions or endeavors, calls us into the fellowship of His Son Jesus Christ. Therefore we are safe; our salvation is assured. "He who began a good work in you, will perfect it until the day of Jesus Christ" (*Philippians 1: 6*). Then, neither humans nor devils, nor governments nor churches, nor kings nor bishops, nor powers celestial, nor powers terrestrial, nor the whole creation itself, "shall be able to separate us from the love of God" (*Romans 8: 39*). They cannot make failure or abortion His plan of salvation. Because God who is faithful is our hope of salvation, in spite of all our unfaithfulness, errors, imperfections, and even of occasional sins and backsliding. (*1 Corinthians 1: 9*).

28   January

Wisdom is the main thing; get wisdom; and with all your effort get understanding. Prize her, and she shall lift you up; she shall bring you to honor when you embrace her. She shall give to your hand an ornament of grace; she shall shield you with a crown of glory.

Proverbs 4: 7–9

Religion and Science

People claim incompatibility between religion and science. But I cannot admit such claim. I shall say that religion is the outcome of scientific research of the spiritual world, while science is the religious observation of the material world. I am not afraid of applying scientific method to the study of religion, nor am I willing to adopt a religious thought that disallow common scientific sense. At the same time, anyone who rejects religious spirit for his scientific study know neither science nor religion. Because, whether in religion or in science, the "Alpha and Omega, the first and the last" (*Revelation 1: 11*) must be an earnest heart, a humble heart, and a heart which loves truth above all.

29   January

My thoughts are not your thoughts, nor your ways My ways, says the LORD. For as the heavens are higher than the earth, so are My ways higher than your ways, and My thoughts than your thoughts.

Isaiah 55: 8–9

Christianity is Revelation

True Christianity is not a religion, but the revelation of God. Religion of this world is human's demanding to gods, but Christianity is God's demanding to humans. Religion puts emphasis on human's efforts, devices, studies, cultivations, logics, training and so forth, whereas Christianity centers the command and grace of God. Ordinary religions approach to gods through various means, whereas Christianity directly enters joy of the grace without means. Thus the difference between religion of this world and the revelation of God is fundamental. The product of this world is completely different form that of God.

30   January

Those who are strong have no need of a physician, but the ones who have illness. I did not come to call the righteous, but sinners to repentance.

Mark 2: 17

Christian, A Sinner

I am a Christian, even though I have no merit of my virtue. The name "Christian" is not a title of honor but a species of sinners. A Christian recognizes the depth of one's sinfulness and clings to the cross of Christ to ask pardon of God. Paul was a Christian; Peter was a Christian. This sounds nowadays a tribute of honor, but in their days, this meant a serious social disgrace to them. Anyone who does not confess before men and women that he or she is a sinner, cannot be a Christian. If anyone who conceives the false notion of a Christian as a civilized wise person does not yet understand the ABC's of Christianity.

31 January

The LORD is near to the broken-hearted; and saves those who are of a contrite spirit. Many are the afflictions of the righteous, but the LORD delivers the person out of them all.

Psalms 34: 18–19

Meaning of Suffering

We suffer various things. And suffering is a necessary condition to purify, train, and make us perfect before God. To our salvation, we may be necessary to suffer domestic problem, illness, lost love, poverty or failure. Each of us may need a specific suffering to be free from one's bondage of sin as we take a specific medicine according to illness. Suffering is not the result of the previous life, but the preparation for other world. It is not punishment but grace. By suffering we are purified to enter the Nation of God and perfected to a Son of God. Rejoice, therefore, for your suffering.

01   February

Stand fast therefore in the liberty wherewith Christ made us free, and be not entangled again with the yoke of bondage.

Galatians 5: 1

Liberty

Liberty is not an inherited right. God, the possessor of prefect liberty, gives us freedom. We can possess true liberty only by the power of God. Tennyson says "Our will is ours to make it Thine." We are made to dedicate our own will to God. Human is of course an indivisible being and not, under any circumstances, to be wholly absorbed into others. A human can lead a nation to true liberty by sacrificing one's own freedom. So a human can attain true liberty by offering one's own freedom to the will of God.

02   February

But let us, who are of the day, be calm, having put on the breastplate of faith and love and the hope of salvation for a helmet.

1 Thessalonians 5: 8

Hope

Hope, faith and love are one in reality. Hope will arise only with faith. And faith is maintained only by hope. Love draws the motive of her activity out of hope, but love without hope, like a lamp extinct of oil, will lose light and heat, and return to the former darkness. Merciless is to coerce love without hope. Faith without hope is stiff-necked and heartless. Hope, indeed, is the most feminine among three sisters. When she stands by love, she will liberate us from the bounds of obligation. By tenderness of hope, faith ceases to be stubborn and becomes gentle. Hope calls down peace from heaven to melt the valley of tears on earth. Hope warms the heart of tears. She opens the heavenly doors to show us deserved glory there.

03   February

You became followers of us, and of the Lord, having received the word in much affliction, with joy of the Holy Spirit. So that you were examples to all that believe in Macedonia and Achaia.

1 Thessalonians 1: 6

Joy in Affliction

There are joy of gaining and losing, of living and dying, and of being beloved and being hated. But the joy of losing is higher than that of gaining; the joy of dying is purer than that of living; the joy of being hated is greater than that of being beloved. Trusting God, we can never lack joy in whatever circumstances we are placed. Only we know that joy in tribulation far exceeds joy in gratification.

04 February

That the blessing of Abraham might come on the Gentiles through Jesus Christ; that we might receive the promise of the Spirit through faith.

Galatians 3: 14

Promise of God

God is faithful. He never betrays anyone believing in Him. He first gives Himself and then the substance of His promise. He first showed Himself to Abraham and then gave the land of Canaan to his numerous sons. The reward of faith is like this, first spirit and then substance. His Spirit will guide a believer to the realization of the promise. We should therefore be patient for not attaining the substance yet. For it is promised by faithful God first. We will at last receive the substance abundantly.

05   February

By faith Abraham obeyed when he was called to go out into a place which he was afterward going to receive for an inheritance. And he went out, not knowing where he went.

Hebrews 11: 8

Adventure of Faith

No life is interesting without venturing; no days is worthy without believing. If all realities are scientifically predicted and everything is mathematically foretold, life will be a mere mechanized being, worthless for living. Yet total mechanization of life shall be impossible as long as life remains alive. Life itself is a great adventure of faith since faith is essential element of life. Faith attempts to make life advance amid heaps of lifeless substances of the universe. Thus we should take adventure of faith.

06   February

Every good gift and every perfect gift is from above, and comes down from the Father of lights, with whom is no changeableness, neither shadow of turning. Of his own will beget he us with the word of truth, that we should be a kind of firstfruits of his creatures.

James 1: 17–18

Good and Evil

Good is to believe in God, and evil is to get away from God and rely on the human self. There is no good or evil other than this. Sickness is not necessarily evil but good as long as it leads us to the Supreme Good. Health is not necessarily good; but it may be evil if it causes us to depend upon ourselves and to account ourselves wise. Same principle is also applied to poverty and wealth. Christ said "Why do you call me good? There is no good but one; that is God" (*Matthew 19: 17*). To look up and face God is good. To depart from and deny God is evil. Distinction between good and evil lies here and nowhere else. This is the distinction of life or death.

07 February

And immediately the Spirit drove Jesus into the wilderness. And He was there in the wilderness forty days.

Mark 1: 12–13

Wondering in Wilderness

The Spirit drove Jesus into the wilderness. God's Spirit drives Jesus' disciples too into the wilderness. A great mission to shoulder, or a great thought to meditate, or a grave doubt to solve, is conferred upon the disciple, so as to force him or her to seek light in solitude. The wilderness may happen to be deep in the mountain, or lonely in the desert or secluded in the monastery. Or the wilderness may be prepared within heart midst the busy and noisy city life, Human's spirit is often tempted by the devil in the wilderness of one's heart. Any Christian shall be driven to the wilderness once in the life. The Christian feels oneself, then, uneasy and unworthy of living. He or she fears and trembles in utter darkness. The heart hears many whisperings. This in fact is the crisis of Christian's life. We should not lose ourselves, even in dense solitude. Know that each and everyone of us is destined to be driven into the wildness once in the life.

08 February

Run to and fro through the streets of Jerusalem, and see now, and know, and seek in her open places, if you can find a person, if there is one who does justice, who seeks the truth; and I will pardon her.

Jeremiah 5: 1

Alone

What if I am the only Christian in the world ? This does not mean that I am the only perfect man in the world. Just the opposite is true that "I am the chief of sinners," and God saved me, or made me a Christian, "that in me first Jesus Christ might show forth all long-suffering, for a pattern to them which should here after believe on him to life everlasting" (*I Timothy 1: 15–16*). If I am the only Christian, it is all very natural that all things in the world appear very strange to me, and I appear very strange to the world. The Christian, I understand, is not a worldly person, and Christianity is not a worldly religion. After all, there are not many Christians in the world, and Christianity is for these very few. As in the time of Isaiah, so now, "only the remnant shall be saved" (*Romans 9: 27*), and "the remnant" means a very small minority. The attempt to make the whole world Christianize is unbiblical and unchristian. Yea, it is an impossible since the world which crucified the Lord Jesus Christ will never become Christian. The world as a whole is essentially anti-Christian, even the so-called Christian nations included. Not because God hates the world, but because the world loves itself, and hates God who is all love.

09   February

You know that Christ was revealed to take away our sins, and in Him is no sin. Whosoever abides in Him does not sin. Whosoever sins has not seen Him nor known Him. Little children, let no one deceive you. A person who does righteousness is righteous, even as that One is righteous. A person who practices sin is of the Devil, for the Devil sins from the beginning. For this purpose the Son of God was revealed, that He might undo the works of the Devil. Whosoever has been born of God does not commit sin, because His seed remains in the person, and the person cannot sin, because the person has been born of God.

1 John 3: 5–9

Rooting out of Sin

Faith sometimes opposes laws; and hope opposes expectations. Yet from faith and hope comes peace that surpasses human understanding. I believe that "God removed sins out of human by Christ." Therefore I no longer worry about my sins, though residue of my sins may still abide in me. For my sins have already rooted out by Christ. The first letter of John truly says: "Christ was revealed to take away our sins ... Whosoever abides in Him does not sin." I firmly believe that Christ rooted out my sins eternally by his crucifixion.

10 February

Like the star, that shines afar,
Without haste and without rest,
Let each person wheel with steady sway,
Round the task that rules the day,
And do one's best.

Goethe: "Without Haste"

Be Slow

Be slow. Take ample time in doing things. Be satisfied with small things. Only do them well. "One who believes shall not make haste" (*Isaiah 28: 16*). God has done for us in His Son what we ought to do for Him. It only remains for us to fill up here and there "that which is lacking of the afflictions of Christ" (*Colossians 1: 24*). The Christian is God Almighty's gentleman or lady; and he or she is not the kind of gentleman or lady who is always in hurry. Salvation has been accomplished for us; the prize has been won; and blessed eternity lies before us. God is working with us, and we with God.

11 February

I did not sit in the circle of mockers, nor rejoice; I sat alone because of Your hand; for You have filled me with indignation.

Jeremiah 15: 17

Serving by Alone

To serve human beings, none of social intercourse will be necessary. We can, but alone, serve human society amply. Everyone is a constituent of humanity. To serve oneself is therefore to serve human beings. By alone one can discover the truth, face God, and have one's inner being purified, so as to step higher and higher to perfection. We can serve ourselves as good examples of humanity to the world. Being alone, life is never a state of doing nothing.

12   February

Then Simon Peter answered Him, Lord, to whom shall we go? You have the words of eternal life. And we have believed and have known that You are the Christ, the Son of the living God.

John 6: 68–69

Christ is My Universe

Christ is my universe. Spiritually I live in Him, am moved by Him and exist for Him. Apart from Him, I can do nothing, as if a monkey falls down from the tree. My misery would be beyond comparison if I were separated from Christ. To follow Christ indeed is the first and last of my living although it is not the gain of my effort. Suffering, contempt, and failure of life will occur around me for the sake of Christ. If there is a life of honor for me, it is to cling to Christ. Miserable yet enviable being I am.

13 February

Jesus said to her, I am the Resurrection and the Life. One who believes in Me, though one die, yet one shall live.

John 11: 25

Resurrection of Christian

A Christian hopes resurrection not by one's own accord but by the Lord Christ's. A Christian never be able to resurrect oneself. But the Lord Jesus Christ restore the life of Christian again; that is, Christ resurrects Himself in the Christian. Christ will abide in a Christian's body and will resurrect him or her also. Where the Spirit of Christ goes, there shall be resurrection; it shall be a natural outcome.

14 February

The Spirit of the Lord Jehovah is on Me; because the LORD has anointed Me to bear the Gospel to the poor; He has sent Me to bind up the broken-hearted, to proclaim liberty to the captives, and the opening of the prison to those who are bound.

Isaiah 61: 1

Silent Missionary

We, as an instrument of God, become His delight and powerful missionary whether in the closed room or in the field. Believing in God deeply and devoutly, we carry out the power of the Gospel without a word or a letter. Because such silent and hidden missionary is always carried out in this world, loud and noisy missionaries can have some fruits. The most powerful missionary is silent missionary, as the Psalm says, "there is no speech nor are there words where their voice is not heard. Their line has gone out through all the earth and their words to the end of the world" (*Psalms 19: 3–4*). Offer yourself to the experiment of the truth, study in deep, suffer seriously, saved from the bottom of the heart, and rejoice from the belly of the mind. You are a delighted missionary of God.

15 February

Now faith, hope, love, these three remain; but the greatest of these is love.

1 Corinthians 13: 13

Faith, Hope and Love

Faith, Hope, and Love, these three are everlasting. All others are temporary and perish. Faith in God is needed all the time. Hope in God's mercy is wanted all the time. And, without Love of God, we die. An everlasting life lives in Faith, Hope, and Love. When these three are integrated into our life, there begins everlasting life. Faith, Hope, and Love exist eternally and equally. But the greatest of these is Love. Just as the God of trinity is integrated into God the Father, so these eternal sisters unite in Love. Stand with Faith; march with Hope; and end with Love. Love is the terminal of human life. Here, human is embraced by God, as His child, and will live forever. "For God is Love" (*I John 4: 8*).

16   February

We are fellow-workers of God, a field-worker of God, and you are a building of God.

1 Corinthians 3: 9

Build Christian Character

Build a Christian character. It is cultivated by the communication with God which means not just mediation or reading the Bible alone, but prayer. Find God's will in the Bible, and perform it with one's faculty given by God in the field, or at the factory or at the shop.

17   February

By grace you are saved through faith, and that not of yourselves, it is the gift of God, not of works, lest anyone should boast. For we are His work, created in Christ Jesus to good works, which God has set that we should walk in good works.

Ephesians 2: 8–10

Mystery of Salvation

False-prophets and false-pastors have told me often that unless I repented of my own accord, God would not be able to save us. Yea, I shall not be saved without my repentance. But repentance comes from God through His Holy Spirit. I have not repented by effort of my own will. This would be entirely beyond my power. But God, abiding in me and transforming my will into His will, prompts me to repent with the power of His will. Never did I repent with my own power. Yet God is gracious enough to accept the repentance on my own. Oh, the mystery of mysteries, it pertains to the mystery of God and His will and also the mystery of salvation. We are not able to explain it philosophically, but we know it is the surest fact pertaining to our will.

18 February

The Nation of Heaven is like to a merchant who is seeking goodly pearls; when he had found one pearl of great price, he went and sold all that he had, and bought it.

Matthew 13: 45–46

Crown Jewel

Sell not the gospel cheap; buy not the gospel cheap. The truth is evaluated by the price paid. Who paid the more will value it the more; who paid the less will value it the less. No one who paid dearly for the gospel has ever abandoned it. An apostate is one who usually bought the gospel cheap.

19 February

Jesus, beholding him, loved him and said to him, One thing you lack. Go, sell whatever you have and give it to the poor, and you shall have treasure in Heaven. And come, take up the cross and follow Me. And he was sad at that saying and went away grieved, for he had great possessions.

Mark 10: 21–22

Crucial Time

God demands us to give up the best we have whether child, or wife, or treasure, or dignity, or worldly fame, or talents and intelligence. Whichever the case is, God demands each of us to give up what we value more than life. This is the crucial time of our faith. Passing this, we are allowed perfectly to be God's possession. Failing this, we are doomed to lose everything hitherto earned. "Life or death," for each of us, is determined at this moment of time.

20 February

They who shall be counted worthy to obtain that world, and the resurrection from the dead, neither marry nor are given in marriage. Nor can they die any more, for they are equal to the angels, and are the children of God, being the sons of the resurrection.

Luke 20: 35–36

Greatest Miracle

Resurrection is a great miracle. A greater miracle is the absolute purification of character. With this greater miracle, the former is no longer a miracle. The fact that Jesus existed indeed is the greatest miracle among miracles. There was a person who had not a bit of flaw in morality; this is already a miracle. And it is natural that resurrection will come upon this very person. Jesus was a person, and yet not a person. To turn inside out; to subdue flesh to spirit, and, in his case, to conquer death with life, He died to resurrect in a higher state of life.

21 February

When I look at Your heavens, the work of Your fingers, the moon and the stars which You have established; I come to ask. What is human that You are mindful of, and the son of man, that You visit him? For You have made human a little lower than the angels, and have crowned the son of man with glory and honor. You made him rule over the works of Your hands.

Psalms 8: 3–6

God and I

There are only two in the Heaven and the World: God and I. God loves me, and I love God. I obey all his voice. I joy when He pleases me. I weep when He anger me. My goal of life is to be righteous before God. I work with Him and share His glory and despise. I am glad when He is praised, and I am angry when He is despised. God takes me to wander of His universe and creatures, and shows all His animals of the field and birds of the air. He grants me to name His creatures, and I name His creatures. I am truly the first Adam in this world. I am alone and there is no one else. Only God is with me. There are only God and I. Therefore I love every person and creature. I joy with God, and everything with Him.

22 February

Circumcised the eighth day, of the stock of Israel, of the tribe of Benjamin, an Hebrew of the Hebrews; as touching the law, a Pharisee; Concerning zeal, persecuting the church; touching the righteousness which is in the law, blameless.

Philippians 3: 5–6

National Christianity

When a Japanese truly and independently believes in Christ, he or she is a Japanese Christian, and his or her Christianity is Japanese Christianity. It is all very simple. A Japanese Christian does not arrogate the whole Christianity to one's self, or does not he or she create a new Christianity by becoming a Christian. He or she is a Japanese, and he or she is a Christian; therefore he or she is a Japanese Christian. A Japanese by becoming a Christian does not cease to be a Japanese. Rather the one becomes more Japanese by becoming a Christians. A Japanese who becomes an American or an Englishman, or an amorphous universal person, is neither a true Japanese nor a true Christian. Paul, a Christian apostle, remained "an Hebrew of the Hebrews" till the end of his life. Savonarola was an Italian Christian, Luther was a German Christian, and Knox was a Scotch Christian. They were not characterless universal persons, but distinctly national, therefore true, Christians.

23   February

The full knowledge of the mystery of God, and of the Father, and of Christ; in whom are hidden all the treasures of wisdom and knowledge.

Colossians 2: 2–3

Cross, Answer of Life

The question of life is unsolvable. No philosophy has ever succeeded in solving it. Good things come to bad persons, and bad things come to good persons. True persons are rejected as hypocrites, and false persons are hailed as saints. The strangest of all things is the life in this world. But one thing that settles all questions is the Cross of Jesus Christ. The Cross solves the question of life, and makes all things clear and comprehensible. The Cross is God's answer to the question of life; it is the key to the enough solution of all the difficult problems of life. Walking in the light of the Cross, we can confront with the biggest inconsistencies of life.

24 February

By night on my bed I sought Him whom my soul loved; I sought Him, but I did not find Him. I will rise now and go about the city, in the streets and in the broad ways; I will seek Him whom my soul loves. I sought Him, but I did not find Him. The watchmen going about the city found me. I said, Have you seen Him whom my soul loves? But a little while after I passed from them, I found Him whom my soul loves.

Song of Solomon 3: 1–4

Soul Seeks Love

A soul demands wholehearted, unselfish, and unbounded love. How tremendous demand a soul makes. The soul cannot be satisfied with a golden palace or heaps of jewels. Soul's thirst of love can never be satiated with finest silks or tastes. Even surrounded by three thousand waiting beauties, the sorrow of a soul hopelessly pants after love. Even a happy home or good friends may not be enough to fill soul's deep-seated yearning of love. What a soul really longs is the love of living and true God, the creator of the whole universe, soul's Friend, soul's Father and soul's Savior. Without this a soul is already dead. With this a soul enters true life of eternal love.

25 February

The scripture has concluded all under sin, that the promise by faith of Jesus Christ might be given to them that believe. But before faith came, we were kept under the law, shut up to the faith which should afterwards be revealed. Wherefore the law was our schoolmaster to bring us to Christ, that we might be justified by faith.

Galatians 3: 22–24

Three Great Moments

A great moment in my life was when I found myself, or rather, was found by God, to be a sinner. For years, my supreme effort was to make myself pure and holy before Him. Another great moment was when I found my righteousness, not in me, but in Him who was crucified for my sins. For years, I tried to realize in myself and others the gospel of Jesus Christ and Him crucified. A third, and perhaps the last great moment in my life was when I was shown that my salvation is not yet, and that when Christ shall appear again, then, and not till then, shall I be like Him. Acknowledgment of sins, salvation by faith, and hope of His coming, were three steps by which my soul was lifted to the joy and freedom of the heavenly vision.

26   February

While we look not at the things which are seen, but at the things which are not seen; for the things which are seen are temporal; but the things which are not seen are eternal.

2 Corinthians 4: 18

Faith and Institution

Churches as we find them in Europe and America are Christian doctrines institutionalized. Institutions are Roman, and doctrines are Greek. But true Christianity is faith, and faith is Hebrew. Political Romans and their European and American descendants have comprehend faith only in forms of institution. Not so the Orientals, who can comprehend faith without forms, and are in this respect akin to Hebrew prophets and Christian apostles. The task of the Orientals in general and of the Japanese in particular is to deinstitutionalize Christianity, and make invisible faith free from visible institutions.

27 February

For as the Father raises the dead and makes alive, even so the Son of man makes alive whomever He will. For the Father judges no man, but has committed all judgment to the Son, so that all should honor the Son, even as they honor the Father. He who does not honor the Son does not honor the Father who sent Him.

John 5: 21–22

Judgment by Christ

God raised Christ to judge us. Judgment, then, is no longer to be feared as we thought. Judgment sounds fearsome when first heard, but thanksgiving, instead of dread, comes when we hear that Christ judges. Christ is the Mediator between God and human and makes defense for human before God, offering atonement of human's sin; He is a gentle Savior and a friend of sinners. God committed judgment to Christ for remission of sin. We are then, notwithstanding the multitude of sins committed, provided with the hope of not guilty. Now we know who judges us, and can therefore stand before Him fearlessly.

28 February

Rejoice evermore. Pray without ceasing. In every thing give thanks; for this is the will of God in Christ Jesus concerning you.

1 Thessalonians 5: 16–18

Give Thanks

Rejoice, give thanks, and look up to a greater blessing. Thanksgiving is an essence of prayer. God never listens to a thankless prayer. "For whoever has, to him shall be given, and he shall have more abundance. But whoever does not have, from him shall be taken away even that which he has" (*Matthew 13: 12*). Gratefulness endorses whosoever has. Anyone who gives thanks will be given more of mercy and blessing; We should not ask to our Father for His mercy by bringing out our "having not." We should rather offer our thanksgiving for His grace.

29 February

Jesus was led by the Spirit up into the wilderness, to be tempted by the Devil. And when He had fasted forty days and forty nights, He was afterwards hungry. And the tempter came to Him.

Matthew 4: 1–3

Trial of Jesus

Oh, Jesus of Nazareth, I thank you for your victory over temptation. I know I will be tried as you were. You were tried every matter of life as we are. Therefore you know well our weakness (*Hebrews 4: 15*). You fought against the devil and you know his strong power. I was caught by the devil, although I wished to serve you. I pray, lead me to your wisdom, give your perception to distinguish the voice of God from the devil. May I have a light to walk your way. May I overcome all temptation to take part in your work of the Nation of Heaven. May I have your glory.

01 March

The word of God is quick, and powerful, and sharper than any two-edged sword, piercing even to the dividing asunder of soul and spirit, and of the joints and marrow, and is a discerner of the thoughts and intents of the heart.

Hebrews 4: 12

Bible and Ethic

The Bible is not a book of ethical law, but a book that witnesses the way to the source of ethic, God. It reveals God's will to humans according to their stage of development. The Bible does not say the slave system should be abolished. But it destroyed the foundation of the slave system by teaching that human is God's son. The Bible does not enforce renunciation of war. But it is turning war as "not-to-be" by teaching the reason why the human soul is so precious. The Bible teaches the fundamentals of ethic, and not its formality. Thus the Bible proves in itself the very words of God.

02 March

Not everyone who says to Me, "Lord, Lord," shall enter the Nation of Heaven, but one who does the will of My Father in Heaven. Many will say to Me in that day, "Lord, Lord, Did we not prophesy in Your name, and through Your name throw out demons, and through Your name do many wonderful works?" And then I will say to them, "I never knew you. Depart from Me, those working iniquity."

Matthew 7: 21–23

Baptism of Heart

Who is a Christian? The baptism and membership of a church does not make a Christian. What makes a Christian is to do God's will and to follow Lord Jesus Christ. It does not matter whatever the form and the name appear outwardly. True baptism comes only from the Holy Spirit, not from the formal ritual of a church. It therefore is baptism of the heart, performed not by human but by God. Human sees outward but God inward. Worldly human seeks outward guarantee of baptism, but a true Christian treasures God's baptism inwardly.

03 March

Blessed are the poor in spirit; for theirs is the Nation of heaven.

Matthew 5: 3

Poor in Spirit

Anyone who wants to be wealthy in heaven must be poor on earth. Poverty shall be of the soul rather than of the flesh. In poverty, one can stand upright and honorable toward Heaven. Such a person is really wealthy spiritually, though poor materially. Poverty is two kinds: external and internal. Spiritual poverty is to account nothing for one's self. Example is Paul the Apostle. He was poor in spirit, having no wisdom to boast of, no virtue to rely on, while behaving, as he confessed, as "the chief of sinners" (*I Timothy 1: 15*). He was, as a matter of fact, humiliated to the uttermost bottom before God; but, by faith in Christ, he was lifted up heavenward in glory.

04   March

By Christ were all things created, that are in heaven, and that are in earth, visible and invisible, whether they be thrones, or dominions, or principalities, or powers; all things were created by him, and for him; And he is before all things, and by him all things consist.

Colossians 1: 16–17

Jesus and Universe

Christ is the center of the universe; Jesus of Nazareth is the revelation of the innermost power of the universe. Love is the power which moves and upholds the universe, and Jesus' love is the highest and deepest and purest one. To say, therefore, that "the universe consists in Him" is conceivable. It reveals that the uniting power of the Pleiades and the Orion originates in this love. Not as a church-dogma, but as a serene transcendental truth we can accept this amazing statement by Paul. Jesus, my savior, is the central power of the universe. Immensity itself is thus brought to a focus in my little heart.

05   March

They came to a place named Gethsemane. And Jesus said to His disciples, ... My soul is exceedingly sorrowful to death. Stay here and watch. And He went forward a little and fell on the ground. And He prayed that, if it were possible, the hour might pass from Him. And He said, Abba, Father, all things are possible to You. Take away this cup from Me. Yet not what I will, but what You will.

Mark 14: 32, 34–36

Sorrow in Gethsemane

Tribulation on Christ's flesh symbolizes His spiritual sorrow. Grace of redemption comes not from His nervous pain but from His spiritual suffering. Not Calvary (where He was crucified) but Gethsemane (where He prayed alone throughout the night before His capture) is the very site where human sins were redeemed. My sins put the crown of thorns upon Christ's head. My sins caused Him to drink a better cup and nailed Him on the cross.

06   March

Commit your way to the LORD; trust also in him; and he shall bring it to pass. And he shall bring forth your righteousness as the light, and your judgment as the noonday. Rest in the LORD, and wait patiently for him.

Psalms 37: 5–7

Submit to God

God lives. He never leaves things as they go. He will, instead of you, accomplish what you should do. It is a truth that God helps those who help themselves. But it is a greater truth that God saves those who submit themselves to Him. Faith does not mean idleness. It means submitting one's own way to God's aid and waiting for its accomplishment. Constant prayer is necessary for this. Watchfulness should not be neglected. We must believe that God's will cannot fail to realize throughout the universe and human history, inasmuch as these are sustained by living God. And thus believing and thus acting, there cannot be any doubt about fruition by God's hand of what we should attain. All believers' peace rests upon the word: "God will do it." Everything shall be done in time as long as we believe and wait.

07   March

A good tree does not bring forth corrupt fruit, neither does a corrupt tree bring forth good fruit.

$$\text{Luke 6: 43}$$

Fruit of Faith

It is evident that the fruit of our faith in Jesus will gradually ripen within. The fruit of faith, as clearly seen, brings about health of body and spirit, as well as an integration of personality. But faith should not at once be take account for its result. Faith alone by its own accord, should be the sole power of salvation. Expecting the result of faith, we will be disappointed. If human can be saved by only the result of one's faith, there will be no hope forever of being saved. Faith as such will bring the unbounded joy of peace within.

08   March

The Father would grant you, according to the riches of His glory, to be strengthened with might by His Spirit in the inner person; that Christ may dwell in your hearts by faith.

Ephesians 3: 16

Love to Christ

We should not inquiry other's faith, like an examiner who tests pupils' understanding, by saying "Do you know this or that?" Faith is not of the knowledge, but of the heart. It is exactly how much we think of Christ. A Believer joys an enduring love to Christ. If not, he or she is an unbeliever. Not the one who comprehends Christianity but the one who loves Christ is a true believer.

09 March

The Lord is the spirit.

2 Corinthians 3: 17

Christ is Spirit

Lord Christ is a particular spirit. His spirit is not "a spirit in human" (*Job 32: 8*), but the spirit to create a new life; that is, the spirit of the inner being. It is an embryo of new life as told "for God's seed remains in him" (*1 John 3: 9*). With this seed planted within, one's spiritual being begins to grow, even into an everlasting life after resurrection and heavenly ascension. This is explained by the Lord as "I am the resurrection, and the (eternal) life" (*John 11: 25*). A Christian's resurrection can only occur with Jesus, yea, in Him alone.

10 March

A prophet is not without honor, except in his own country and in his own house.

Matthew 13: 57

Be Great

Be great; so great that neither you know your greatness, nor the world recognize it. Be great as the sun which simply shines and makes no noise, and which the world recognizes only when it ceases to shine, as in the Arctic winter or the tropical rainy season. Be great like God Himself, who is almost forgotten by humankind, and whose existence is a problem, not to be proved even by great philosophers like Descartes and Kant. Oh, be great and common as the air and the sun-light, ignored and unrecognized.

11   March

They shall put you out of the congregation. The time is coming that everyone who kills you will think that he bears God service. And they will do these things to you because they have not known the Father nor Me. But I have told you these things so that when the time shall come you may remember that I told you of them.

John 16: 2–4

Persecution

Christ said, "the time is coming that everyone who kills you will think that he bears God service." They persecute us because they believe we are wrong. Their oppression, then, is based on a cause that calls for our great sympathy. They want to kill us for the sake of righteousness, or the sake of society, humanity, yea, in some cases, for the very cause of Christianity, they try to kill us. Their anger, therefore, holds a grain of sincerity to be admired. We should not blame, but pray for them.

12   March

Peace I leave with you, My peace I give to you. Not as the world gives do I give to you. Let not your heart be troubled, neither let it be afraid.

John 14: 27

Brave and Integral Life

There is a gift that everyone can leave for next generations. That is a brave and integral life. Not everybody can leave the gift of money, writings, institution, property and other achievements. But one's brave and integral life is the only one that everybody can leave as a gift for next generations. Then what is the brave and integral life? It is to believe that the world is God's dominion not devil's and that there is hope in the world and not despair. And it is to walk in the world believing that the world is meaningful and not meaningless. Leave one's brave and integral life as the gift for next generations.

13 March

It is better to trust in the LORD than to trust in humans. It is better to trust in the LORD than to trust in princes.

Psalms 118: 8–9

Trust in God Alone

Trust in God, and not in human. Reliance upon God far excels dependence on dignitaries and nobles. One shall be disappointed in humans and ashamed of the notables who intertwine love with hate, interchange laud with libel time and again. Not so with Jehovah, the unchangeable rock of eternity. He affords shelter for the decaying, and support for the dying. By Him, darkness will turn to light; weakness will change to mercy. Nothing of shame with Him. As the sun increases glory to reach the heights of noon, our life advances from glory to glory, as the years go on, to reach the height of heavenly joy. Neither wealth, fame, rank, or medals can console us, Jehovah alone heals our solitude.

14   March

I saw a new heaven and a new earth; for the first heaven and the first earth were passed away; ... And God shall wipe away all tears from their eyes; and there shall be no more death, neither sorrow, nor crying, neither shall there be any more pain; for the former things are passed away.

Revelation 21: 1, 4

New Heaven and New Earth

For us, Christians, death means going to his Lord. Joy accompanies it, instead of fear. We leave flesh to see the Lord face to face, whom we served invisibly by faith. By this, death gives us an image of going back to our homeland. It must be joyful and grateful. Reunion with our Lord means reunion with our beloved. Through death we do not go astray in nowhere. We go to a land of our friends. There we shall have the most intimate communion, without prejudice or grievance. There we enjoy wholehearted exchange of love. Yea, just beyond the stream of death, we see yonder this paradise of love.

15   March

But Jesus called them and said, Allow the little children to come to Me, and forbid them not. For of such is the Nation of God.

Luke 18: 16

Simple Faith

Believe simply. Charity comes with simplicity. Zeal comes with simplicity. Belief cannot be zealous if one puzzles over many problems and doctrines. Seek simplicity of faith first, then the rests shall follow. In Japan, Buddhism spread into all strata of the people when Honen (1178–1215) compressed the doctrine into six words "I believe in the Savior Buddha." Nichiren (1201–1261) also realizing this, condensed his faith into nine words "I believe in the Law of the Lotus Sutra." His simplicity penetrated to the land of Japan with a great extent. There is nothing so incompetent as a complex belief. I am ease of mind within, and proclaim my faith clearly without, as long as I express my belief in the fewest solid words.

16   March

We are troubled on every side, yet not distressed; we are caught up, but not in despair; Persecuted, but not forsaken; cast down, but not destroyed; Always bearing about in the body the dying of the Lord Jesus, that the life also of Jesus might be made revealed in our body.

2 Corinthians 4: 8–10

Die to One's Self

To work for God, I must first die to myself. Otherwise I may find myself imbued with the spirit of self-love and self-protection. I can live with God only upon dying to myself. Then, I can have clear conscience, freed from fear. For announcing the gospel of God, I have no anxiety of politics or any matter to disturb my work. The world tries to assimilate me; but I am in no way to surrender or compromise to the world. Though the whole world may stand there in united and unison, I will stand here alone. I will abide in the evergreen, defining frost or snow land. I will stand solid by the immovable spirit of a mighty mountain. My being shall light up millions, and my voice shall calm billions. Only by living with God, can addressing first yield the fruit for the world.

17　March

The word of the cross is foolishness to those who perish; but to us who are saved, it is the power of God.

1 Corinthians 1: 18

Salvation of Soul

How could my soul be saved? Christianity would be foolish without this yearning. Christianity is not a sect of philosophy like Buddhism nor a device for drilling self-power like "Zen." Christianity is the power of God to save our souls. The Advent of Christ and His redemption of sin on the cross are the acts of God to save our souls. These occurrences, therefore, shall be understood only for the salvation of the souls.

18   March

When Gideon perceived that he was the LORD, Gideon said, Alas, O Lord GOD. For because I have seen the LORD face to face. And the LORD said to him, Peace be to you; fear not; You shall not die.

Judges 6: 22–23

God of Gideon

Gideon needs not fear; he shall not die. Jehovah did not appear to him to kill him, but to save him and, by him, to save his house and country. Moreover, Jehovah appeared to him not as the God of domination but as the God of salvation of human race. He governs the whole universe; authority and power are in His hand. But when He comes to the world to save human, He put on humility and did appear a figure like a man. Jehovah is God who speaks to human. First He appeared to Moses, telling him of His name Jehovah (*Exodus 3: 13*); and later, as Jesus Christ, to the world to redeem the sins of the whole humanity.

19 March

O death, where is your sting? O grave, where is your victory? The sting of death is sin; and the strength of sin is the law. But thanks be to God, which gives us the victory through our Lord Jesus Christ.

1 Corinthians 15: 55–57

Sin and Death

Spirit and flesh are originally united into one. But, as a result of sin, human underwent the sad separation between the spirit and the flesh in the life. This is a most grievous thing just like a criminal being hanged. We not only dislike death but fear it greatly, because we know we human beings are invariably sentenced to death as the punishment for our sins. Death is seeded in a misery flesh because of our sin. Oh, who is there that does not fear death? And, who is there that does not seek resurrection? If death has to be met once as a result of the sentence of sin, why not the hope to be given a new body as a result of the remission of sin? Isn't this a yearning and earnest hope at the bottom of the human heart?

20 March

Do not be unequally yoked together with unbelievers; for what fellowship does righteousness have with unrighteousnesses? And what communion does light have with darkness? ... Therefore come out from among them and be separated

2 Corinthians 6: 14, 17

Keep Purity of Faith

If, as a child of God, one wishes to keep the purity of one's faith permanently, the one should withdraw oneself in holy solitude in order to avoid the sin and impurity of this-worldly human relationships as far as possible. In contrast, one will no longer be a child of God, if one endeavor to enlarge of one's scope of social intercourse, to increase of one's own power by means of worldly powers, to seek one's friends among the unbelievers, and to get tied up with the notables of the world. The one is like the salt lost its flavor and will be cast out by both God and humans. Children of God should keep themselves in holy seclusion. Remember that the great fall of human started with the error of the children of God in the intercourse with humans.

21 March

You are the salt of the earth, but if the salt loses its savor, with what shall it be salted? It is no longer good for anything, but to be thrown out and to be trodden underfoot by humans.

Matthew 5: 13

Salt of Earth

Earthly life is fast to deteriorate. Its freshness is short and its liveliness is temporary. Life on earth gets rotten in an instant and hardened without waiting. Here is the necessity of salt to preserve the existing virtues, to enhance their fairness and thereby to encourage goodness of the earth. This need on earth is to be filled by Christians who hold God's living words in their hearts and souls. By Christians indeed, all the virtues even outside of the gospel, yea, all the good outside of the faith, shall be maintained, purified and wide-spread. This is an indisputable fact. The old ethics and old faiths are thus, in a true sense, revived by the gospel of Christ.

22 March

And now, Israel, what does the LORD your God require of you, but to fear the LORD your God, to walk in all His ways, and to love Him, and to serve the LORD your God with all your heart and with all your soul, to keep the commandments of the LORD, and His statutes, which I command you today for your good?

Deuteronomy 10: 12–13

Live with God

When my heart feels devoid of love, I have to realize God does not abide in my heart. When my heart fears, I have to realize God does not live with me. When I lack true perception, being unable to appreciate the universe and life, I have to realize my eyes are shut to God. When I feel joyless, powerless, hopeless and as if trudging heavily laden, I have to realize I am walking alone apart from God. This is not only in my own case but in nations and societies as well. No living virtue and no burning hope can exist if a person does not live with God and keep afar from God. Thus, to live with God is of primary importance, not only to myself but also to my fellows and nations.

23 March

When I do judge, My judgment is true; for I am not alone, but I and the Father who sent Me.

John 8: 16

Power of Independence

Independence should not necessarily mean refusal of others' aid, but full practice of all inner power of one's own. A human being is a miniature universe. Within oneself a person can find almost limitless store of power. When this power is fully utilized, the person will be able not only to fulfill one's righteous demand but also to willingly help others to an extent more than needed. In contrast, relying on others comes from ignorance of one's inner power and makes the person weak. We become want by relying on others. Thus dependence is not just a weakness but a sin. And independence is not only a virtue but an imperative duty.

24 March

You know the Spirit of God; every spirit that confesses that Jesus Christ has come in the flesh is of God.

1 John 4: 2

Three Great Truths

The first great truth is that God is not just Power but Love, a Loving Father. The whole universe wears a different appearance when viewed with faith in the Father of Love. The second great truth is that Jesus Christ is not just a man, not even the greatest man, but God himself. Peace that passes all understandings is ours when we come to believe in the divinity of Jesus. The third great truth is that the Holy Spirit is not an influence, but a person. Faith becomes real, and true freedom is won only when we realize the Personality of the Holy Spirit.

25 March

It is of the LORD'S mercies that we are not consumed, because his compassions fail not. They are new every morning; great is your faithfulness.

Lamentations 3: 22–23

New Every Morning

The Lord's mercies are new day by day. Especially they are fresh every morning. The best thought comes in the morning; the loveliest song tunes in the morning; birds sing aloud in the morning; and Jesus resurrected in the morning. The earth, in fact, dies every night and resurrects every morning. God abides with us always, but particularly teaches us in the morning. We should therefore preserve especially the morning thoughts. Neither should we miss the morning whispers. "They are new every morning." Yea, the old gospel, like the old earth, is new every morning. And our joy reaches its zenith in the morning of resurrection.

26   March

Jesus says to them, Truly, truly, I say to you, unless you eat the flesh of the Son of man, and drink His blood, you do not have life in you. Whoever partakes of My flesh and drinks My blood has eternal life, and I will raise them up at the last day.

John 6: 53–54

Power of Christ

Jesus Christ said: "All power is given to me in heaven and in earth" (*Matthew 28: 18*). He revived a dead man while on earth, performed various miracles, proved to be the greatest historical power in elevating humanity, and caused an otherwise impossible inner change in the believers' hearts. Jesus Christ is truly the Son of God, the Lord of humans, the Savior of us. The Lord Jesus Christ resurrects the dead, as He said "I am the life and the resurrection" (*John 11: 25*). There is nothing mysterious about it.

27 March

But I commanded them this thing, saying, Obey My voice, and I will be your God, and you shall be My people; and walk in all the ways that I have commanded you, so that it may be well with you.

Jeremiah 7: 23

Walk with God

"Walk" means "walk quietly," and not to fly, run, but to walk. It is not to attempt a great leap, a wild dash, or a crazy moving but to rely on God quietly and to fulfill His will patiently. Not to attempt a great enterprise, a marvelous missionary work, nor to try to exhibit a wonderful miracle; but to live a life simply obeying God's command, following His word, and believing that one's life-work is to be faithful to God. The greater part of life of faith is patience, quietness and hope. Living with God is a life of appreciation with what God has given.

28   March

In those days they shall say no more, The fathers have eaten a sour grape, and the children's teeth are set on edge. But every one shall die for one's own iniquity.

                                        Jeremiah 31: 29–30

New Generations

A human is born into the world as an entirely new creature. He or she gets nothing of moral inheritance from his or her ancestors. An evil father may beget a good person, a feeble mother may give birth to a stout child. God renews His work with each and every individual. Nobody need be afraid of the stains of one's inheritance. Everyone is directly created by God like Adam and Eve. The cry of the newborn baby is the voice for new creature. Hope is pressing on to the world day by day, why not keep aloof from fear of accumulate corruptions.

29 March

He who has begun a good work in you will complete it until the day of Jesus Christ.

Philippians 1: 6

Ongoing Salvation

Anyone who scorns of the imperfection of creatures, slanders God, ridicules Christians, rejects the Gospel. They just see God's work halfway, but do not view it in its coming completion. Salvation started, but has not been finished yet; it is on the way to perfection. When completed, it will be, "Eye has not seen, nor ear heard, neither have entered into the heart of human" (*1 Corinthians 2: 9*). We, believers, therefore should wait to see it completed.

30 March

If we confess our sins, He is faithful and just to forgive us our sins, and to cleanse us from all unrighteousness.

1 John 1: 9

Savior of Soul

Christ is neither a physician nor a politician. His mission is to save souls, and there is no equal among the human race in this respect. The savior of souls is the person who forgives soul's sins and gives restful joy to one's conscience. Neither a moralist nor a philosopher could become such a one. No matter how respectable a person may be in virtue, good deeds or wisdom, the one cannot redeem and pardon the sin of a soul. What a soul needs is the spiritual existence who can redeem the sin of the soul. And Christ did it. Thus as long as we live in the soul and spirit, we need for the advent of Christ and for the work He did.

31 March

Therefore we were buried with Him by baptism into death, so that as Christ was raised up from the dead by the glory of the Father; even so we also should walk in newness of life. For if we have been joined together in the likeness of His death, we shall also be in the likeness of His resurrection.

Romans 6: 4–5

Resurrection of Jesus

I believe that my Savior resurrected from death. We killed a righteous Man and believed He was dead. Why not strike the Himalayas and believe them broken down? But my Beloved never died. Nature evolves itself; how can God despise His own creation? His flesh may have decayed; the linen around His corpse may have turned into soil. But His heart, His love, His courage, and His faithfulness never perish with His flesh. I do not know how, in what form and where to see Him again, but "Love does dream, Faith does trust Somehow, somewhere meet we must" (*Whittier J. G.*).

01   April

The winter is past, the rain is over and gone; The flowers appear on the earth; the time of the singing of birds is come, and the voice of the turtle is heard in our land; The fig tree put forth her green figs, and the vines with the tender grape give a good smell. Arise, my love, my fair one, and come away.

Song of Solomon 2: 11–13

Song of Spring

Arise, my love, my fair one, my hope, my savior, and come out from your tomb. Lo, the winter of shame has past; the spring of glory is come. The rain is over and gone. The black wind of anger, suspicion and jealousy will no longer overtake you. The time of the singing of birds is come. The voices of the turtle, the lark and the bunting are heard in our field. The fig tree is budding in pink the full bloom of cherry blossoms is near at hand. The vines with the tender grape give a good smell; all the woodland is starting to deck herself with gorgeous dresses. Arise, my love, my fair one, my hope, my savior, and come out from your tomb. Vanquish your enemy with love; quench your anger with grace. Let there come forth a spring of charity over the world, like the field already tinted with spring.

02 April

The time is coming, and now is, when the true worshipers shall worship the Father in spirit and truth, for the Father seeks such to worship Him. God is a spirit, and they who worship Him must worship in spirit and in truth.

John 4: 23–24

Faithfulness

One knows God with believing in Him. If one doubts Him from the outset, God will be an eternal mystery. Faithfulness is indispensable for knowing God, because we know God is faithful. A person of faith dismisses most of what others suspect of Him. Faith demands faithfulness. Faith disclose its hidden treasures to the one who approaches by faithfulness. Faith keeps rigid silence against skepticism, closing its doors tightly against unfaithful approaches. If skepticism comes near, faith will say "Oh, get away from here. I have nothing to give you." The faithful will be foolish if viewed in doubt. To the eyes of skepticism, faith is a childish or nonsense matter. This is the fate of a person of faithfulness; the more so is the faithful of God.

03 April

And about the ninth hour Jesus cried with a loud voice, saying, Eli, Eli, lama sabachthani? That is to say, My God, my God, why have You forsaken me?

Matthew 27: 46

Religion is Personal

Religion is personal, not general. It is not "we," but "I," not plural, but singular person. It is not humankind or humanity, but I myself. "My God, My God, why have You forsaken Me" was Jesus' own religion. "O wretched man that I am. Who shall deliver me out of the body of this death?" (*Romans 7: 24*) was Paul's religion. Theologians seeking after general truth of religion, never find it. God is found only in one's inmost soul; and a person who cannot make oneself an object-lesson in religion, can never be its preacher. Modern Christianity is tasteless and powerless, chiefly because it is general and social, and not personal and individual. Is there anyone more useless than the "expert" in religion under heaven?

04 April

Let this mind be in you, which was also in Christ Jesus; Who, being in the form of God, thought it not robbery to be equal with God; But made himself of no reputation, and took upon him the form of a servant, and was made in the likeness of humans; And being found in manner as a human, he humbled himself, and became obedient to death, even the death of the cross.

Philippians 2: 5–8

Humbleness

Humbleness is a fine virtue. But it should not be an intentional attempt, which may be called a humbleness in appearance. In most cases, a "humble concession" or a "humble resignation" does not mean humbleness out of one's own heart, but merely to cover one's own defects or to demonstrate one's pretended humbleness. True Humbleness is not always praiseworthy; it is to be empty-handed before God. It works into nobleness of personality unconsciously. True Humbleness is attained only by one who empties one's self in Christ Jesus.

05   April

This is a faithful saying, and worthy of all acceptation, that Christ Jesus came into the world to save sinners; of whom I am chief. But for this cause I obtained mercy, that in me first Jesus Christ might show forth all long-suffering, as a pattern to those being about to believe on Him to life everlasting.

1 Timothy 1: 15–16

Am I Christian?

I am a Christian only in the sense that I am a chief of sinners, and am what I am by the grace of God. In any other sense, I am not a Christian. I am not a member of any church, a Catholic or a Protestant. I do not have any set of dogmas formulated by theologians. I am not supported by any one of innumerable Christian institutions. If I am a Christian at all, I am a Christian only in my innermost soul. Outwardly, I am as unrelated and unprivileged as any heathen. And I am churchly a "Gentile" (*Matthew 4: 15*) and a "publican" (*Matthew 9: 10–11*).

06   April

Listen, O coast lands, to Me; and listen, lend your ear, peoples from afar; the LORD has called Me from the womb; He has made mention of My name from My mother's bowels. And He has made My mouth like a sharp sword; in the shadow of His hand He has hidden Me, and made Me a polished shaft. He has hidden Me in His quiver, and said to Me, You are My servant.

Isaiah 49: 1–3

No Imitation

I do not imitate Augustine, or Luther, or Knox, or Wesley, or Carlyle, or any other man of past and present. I am what I am; God made me for a special purpose, placed me in a special position, and appointed me a special work. God leads me in special ways, because I am His special instrument. They who compare me to this and that man in Europe and America, misrepresent me and misunderstand God's creation of me. God makes no two humans the same, and every person is His special handiwork. In that I was individually made, and am individually led by my God, am I a free and independent man. I look to Him for His individual guidance day by day, in ways which He cut out for me. I am alone, but not alone, for God walks with me.

07   April

When you heard the word of us, you received it as the Word of God, not as the word of humans. The Word of God truly works in you who believe.

                                                1 Thessalonians 2: 13

Best Commentary on Bible

The best commentary on the Bible is not Augustine's, not Calvin's, not any others', but one's experience of life itself. Without this, no vastness of knowledge, or no height of culture is sufficient to reach the depth of the Biblical truth. With one's experience, mere ability to read the alphabet is sufficient to know God's truth in the Bible. Driven out of the church, persecuted by fellow citizens, betrayed by friends, I can now realize what the cross, the gift of Christianity, means. The Bible is the Scripture of God because it is not a book of knowledge, but of one's experience.

08 April

The LORD shall judge the people; judge me, Oh LORD, according to my righteousness, and according to my integrity within. Oh let the wickedness of the wicked come to an end, but establish the just. For the righteous God tries the minds and hearts. My defense is from God, who saves the upright in heart.

Psalms 7: 8–10

God is Righteous

God is righteous. He fulfills his righteousness in this world without fail. But when and how will it be done? This is beyond human comprehension. The time and method of perfecting righteousness are entirely in God's will. We cannot know His will by our understanding. Desire to grasp His will disturbs our peace of mind. "Now faith is the substance of things hoped for the evidence of things not seen" (*Hebrew 11: 1*). Believe earnestly in God's righteousness and wait quietly for its fulfillment; this is an ideal attitude of a Christian life.

09 April

Truly I say to you, That whosoever shall say to this mountain, Be removed, and be cast into the sea; and shall not doubt in one's heart, but shall believe that those things which one says shall come to pass; one shall have whatsoever one says.

Mark 11: 22–24

Faith and Miracle

A miracle is a matter of faith, not of reason. Faith does not determine a miracle; but first faith comes and miracle follows. A miracle can only exist with faith. There will be a miracle under God's mercy, when we courageously, with faith, follow Gods' command. Never say "My power fails to do a miracle"; Almighty God does it. God uses my faith and courage to tear asunder the stubborn heart of the aged. God speaks a few simple words through my mouth to lead my brethren and friends to repentance. Nothing is done while one cowardly hesitates many a chance of doing miracle. Have faith and be courageous.

10 April

Blessed are you, when people shall scold you, and persecute you, and shall say all manner of evil against you falsely, for my sake. Rejoice, and be exceeding glad; for great is your reward in heaven; for so persecuted they the prophets which were before you.

Matthew 5: 11–12

Grace of Suffering

Who says suffering is a divine punishment? Who says it is a retribution for sins committed in one's previous birth? For us, believers, suffering is the greatest blessing. It is the only way to know Christ. Only by suffering, are we enabled to communicate with Him heart to heart. Only by climbing steps, one by one, of suffering, we are brought into the Nation of our Heavenly Father. Come then freely on me, suffering and tribulation. They shall be welcome to me.

11 April

Have I not commanded you? Be strong and of good courage. Do not be afraid, neither be dismayed. For the LORD your God is with you in all places where you go.

Joshua 1: 9

God with You

John Wesley, the founder of Methodism, told his friends several times, on the day prior to his death, "The very best thing, beyond comparison, is that God be with us." God is the supremely good and most precious treasure that a person, governing all creatures, can associate with. God is above property, above physical health, and is my companion above my family. Wealth may be stolen or wasted; the nation, the Church and friends may forsake me; an enterprise will drive me bankruptcy; my flesh shall be perish sooner or later. But amid all these courses of life, I can hold fast to God for ever and ever. Nobleness of human can best be defined as that it should not be satisfied with anything less than God Almighty.

12   April

I am Joseph your brother, whom you sold into Egypt. Now therefore be not grieved, nor angry with yourselves, that you sold me hither; for God did send me before you to preserve life. ... So now it was not you that sent me hither, but God; and he has made me a father to Pharaoh, and lord of all his house, and a ruler throughout all the land of Egypt.

Genesis 45: 4–5, 8

Joseph's Life

Circumstances will get out of the question as long as Jehovah abides with us. All circumstances are meant to show forth His glory. "The righteous has many sufferings, but the LORD deliveries the one out of them all" (*Psalms 34: 19*). Jehovah will give the righteous a spirit of honesty and industry to rescue the one. The environment itself opens a way of salvation. We need not to worry about our surroundings. At the appointed place and with diligence, honesty and faithfulness, one can find a way of salvation providentially. Joseph, a beloved son of Jacob, received a blessed life from God, though no miracle took place for him. He established himself along the way of upright life. A life of plainness, guided by Jehovah, is indeed a miracle of miracles.

13 April

God has blessed us in all wisdom and prudence; Having made known to us the mystery of His will, according to His goodness which He has purposed in Himself; . . We are predestinated according to the purpose of Him who works all things after the counsel of His own will

Ephesians 1: 8–9, 11

God's Plan

God fulfills His will regardless the enterprise of humans. He is an absolute dictator, who created all creatures and humans and carries out His plan. Humans are created for God; not God is for humans. All creatures in heaven and earth are created for God, not for humans. Therefore the purpose of a human is to fulfill God's will, not to enjoy one's happiness of life. It does not matter for me whether I am fortunate or not, since I know the true meaning of my existence. The mission of my life is to take part in the work of God. The task is to fulfill the plan of God, otherwise I myself is nothing. My glory is as a co-worker of God. I should not have self-interest, or my sole interest is to fulfill God's plan.

14 April

Behold, I will lure her and bring her into the wilderness, and speak comfortably to her. And I will give her vineyards to her from there, and the valley of tear for a door of hope. And she shall sing there, as in the days of her youth, and as in the day when she came up out of the land of Egypt.

Hosea 2: 14–15

Wilderness of Life

The wilderness is a desolately place where no person lives. It represents a state of loneliness. Failure of enterprise, impaired fame, separation of near and dear beloved by death; these are the wilderness of life. In such wilderness God will guide His beloved to give them the words of comfort. Human in the garden of this world is pleased to listen to the human voice rather than to God's. But, like Elijah, one who had to wander out alone into the wilderness hears the small still voice of God (*1 Kings 19: 12*). The first step of salvation must be the trials in the wilderness. There the sins of ours are revealed; there an approach to God is granted; there the voice of God is heard; and then our salvation is to begin.

15   April

Love does not envy, does not boast, is not puffed up; does not behave indecently, does not seek her own, is not easily provoked, thinks no evil. Love does not rejoice in iniquity, but rejoices in the truth.

1 Corinthians 13: 5–6

Love Envies Not

Love envies not. Love completes by itself and therefore does not need to envy other's success or to be jealous of other's superiority. The wealthy may have strife; the learned and the religious may burn with jealousy; but anyone fulfilled with love is not disordered by the ill thoughts of suspicion and envy. Love brings about a living fountain. It knows giving but not taking. Being self-sufficient, it is not bothered by hearing of other's luxury. In love, the poor does not want to be the rich, and the ignorant does not envy the intellect; love makes the ultimate good and beauty of life. With love thus, one will cut all the self-desires apart. With gold in hand, one will not be envious of holders of copper, iron or lead. Similarly, with love in heart, one cannot be envious of other's talents of body, intellect, wealth, or social intercourse. Love envies not, yea, only upon attaining the love of God, can we be able to rise above the level of jealousy.

16   April

My brothers, take the prophets who have spoken in the name of the Lord, for an example of suffering of evil, and of patience. Behold, we count blessed those who endure. You have heard of the patience of Job, and you have seen the end of the Lord, that the Lord is full of compassion and of loving-kindness.

James 5: 10–11

Works of Suffering

We are not allowed to escape from suffering; we are destined to suffer. And we are saved from suffering and afflictions. God lets fire to burn out the impurity whatsoever is remaining within us. And then, God saves us out of ashes. Tribulation cannot be overcome by escaping. Let suffering devour us first to overcome it by true salvation. Death can only be conquered by death (*Hebrew 2: 14*). Sorrow can be overcome only when we come through sorrow. God saves us out of afflictions; yes, out of miseries, and perfectly.

17 April

Abraham stretched out his hand and took the knife to slay his son. And the voice of Jehovah came to him from the heavens and said, Abraham. Abraham. And he said, Here am I. And He said, Do not lay your hand on the lad, nor do anything to him. For now I know that you fear God, since you have not withheld your son, your only one, from Me. And Abraham lifted up his eyes, and looked. And, behold, a ram behind him was entangled in a thicket by its horns. And Abraham went and took the ram and offered it up for a burnt offering instead of his son.

Genesis 22: 10–13

Spirit of Sacrifice

Jehovah is God of mercy. He requires His children sacrifice not for the sake of sacrifice, but for their own sins. A voice from heaven came to Abraham when he was going to sacrifice his beloved son: "Lay not your hand upon the lad." Oh, salvation has come. His beloved son, once offered to God, was given back to him. Here, Abraham, came to realize what a sacrifice should be. A sacrifice does not mean throwing away, but gaining again. The object of the burnt offering was provided separately by God Himself.

18 April

If anyone says, I love God, and hates one's brother, The one is a liar. For if one does not love one's brother whom one has seen, how can one love God whom one has not seen?

1 John 4: 20

Orthodoxy

Love brethren with the heart of Christ. True orthodoxy of Christianity is to love your neighbor within Christ, not to confess any creed. If we fall short of Christ's love, charity, long-suffering and patience, we are not true His followers. Our faith should be questioned if it does not transform us into an image of Christ. Before confirming our faith, we should first become meek and gentle in heart like Christ.

19   April

These things have I written to you that believe on the name of the Son of God; that you may know that you have eternal life, and that you may believe on the name of the Son of God.

1 John 5: 13

Faith in God and Eternal Life

Without faith in God and everlasting life, there comes out nothing great, neither great sorrow nor great joy, neither great suffering nor great peace, neither great lamentation nor great praising. Without deep faith in God and everlasting life, none of the great literature will come forth, nor a great revolution will be realized. Lacking faith in these two, life will be nonsense and empty. Upon only faith in these two, Augustine constructed theology, Dante composed "Divine Comedy," Luther initiated the Reformation, and Cromwell established the Commonwealth. A great one is nobody but the one who fears God instead of human, and who trusts in the life to come instead of hoping in this world. Being worldly does not make a great person. A truly great person is only made when the one becomes conscious as a person of God and rests upon the conviction of eternal life.

20 April

God has revealed them to us by His Spirit; for the Spirit searches all things, yea, the deep things of God. For who knows the things of a person except the spirit of one's self? So also no one knows the things of God except the Spirit of God.

1 Corinthians 2: 10–11

Human Spirit

Oh, unfathomable spirit. Spirit is not form, not appearance, not knowledge, not circumstances, not heredity, not action, and not morality. Spirit is living personality in the depth of a person. "The inward part of human and the heart are deep" (*Psalms 64: 6*). God's spirit alone can know the human spirit. One cannot comprehend it by searching from outside. This is why human cannot judge human. Therefore, the Bible says, "The Lord does not see as human does. For human looks on the outward appearance, but the Lord looks on the heart" (*1 Samuel 16: 7*).

21 April

Knowing that a person is not justified by the works of the law, but by the faith of Jesus Christ, even we have believed in Jesus Christ, that we might be justified by the faith of Christ, and not by the works of the law; for by the works of the law shall no flesh be justified.

Galatians 2: 16

Justification by Faith

Faith seeks its ground on Christ and His cross alone. This faith requires neither its worldly success as proof nor its own sanctity. True faith is simple faith. This faith depends not on social work or morality but only on Jesus Christ and His cross. As Columbus ventured upon his voyage without any landmark to guide him, but simply relying upon the stars in heaven, so is our faith to be. And, only in this faith, we can withstand against the world, without being afraid of humanhood and sin. With courageous faith, we journey our ship not to the New Continent but to the New Jerusalem.

22 April

Arise, shine; for your light has come, and the glory of the LORD has risen on you. For behold, the darkness shall cover the earth, and gross darkness the peoples; but the LORD shall rise on you, and His glory shall be seen on you.

Isaiah 60: 1–2

Darkness and Hope

With all the progress in science and art of living, the world is ever darker than before. And churches and governments, by all their means of enlightenment, are totally incompetent to dispel the darkness. But we are not discouraged with this darkness. Rather our confidence grows by this very darkness because "the Lord shall arise" upon us, and "His glory shall be seen" upon us. Not by evolution, nor by efforts of humans, but by the power of God shall the world and humankind be perfected. The Word of God stands sure and shall not return to Him empty. Hallelujah to the Highest.

23   April

Therefore being justified by faith, we have peace with God through our Lord Jesus Christ;

Romans 5: 1

Peace in Faith

Simple faith does not calculate on its result. Faith that stands for its own sake can alone bring a person true peace. This is the peace spoken of by Christ as "My peace I give to you" (*John 14: 27*). This is the peace written by Paul as "the peace of God, which passes all understanding" (*Philippians 4: 7*). This is a deep, strong, and solid faith. With this faith a Christian can conquer the world. Faith in God's righteousness reveals its power beyond the practices of the law; this faith alone can bring about a great business, a great literature, a great art, a great politician and a great country; in short, this faith alone can transform the society fundamentally.

24 April

Where is the wise? Where is the scholar? Where is the defender of this world? Has not God made foolish the wisdom of this world? For since, in the wisdom of God, the world by wisdom did not know God, it pleased God by the foolishness of preaching to save those who believe.

1 Corinthians 1: 20–21

Democracy and Christ

The world is saved by Christ, not by democracy. Democracy at best is a political principle of human power but spiritually powerless. The world is saved not by a principle, but by a person; not by the sum of persons, but by an almighty, all-knowing, all-loving person. The resurrected, living Christ is the only hope of the world. He alone, who is able even to subject all things to Himself, can recreate the world into a new earth wherein dwells the righteous. The salvation of the world will come not from democracy but from Christ, not from the reformation but from the recreation, not from the United Nations but from gathering of all nations at the feet of the coming Christ for judgment and guidance. And there is no other.

25 April

The entrance of Your words gives light; it gives understanding to the simple.

Psalms 119: 130

Bible Study

Christianity is with the Bible, though it is not equal to the Bible. A Christian learns the Bible. The study of the Bible is a necessary way to become a Christian, although it does not always lead to a Christian. This path should be the same among different sects, denominations and even apostates as well. Bible study is the best way of missionary and of learning the world knowledge. The best solid faith arises from Bible study. Sincere study of the Bible is beneficial even for public goods. Do not limit Bible study just for a means of church propaganda.

26 April

It happened when Jephthah saw his daughter, he tore his clothes and said, Alas, my daughter. You have brought me very low, and you are one of those who trouble me. For I have opened my mouth to the LORD, and I cannot go back. And she said to him, My father, you have opened your mouth to the Lord; do to me according to that which has come out of your mouth.

Judges 11: 35–36

Life is Sacrifice

Happiness is not the most important goal of life. Duty is more precious than happiness. We should give up happiness for the cause of duty. The cost of duty which we sacrifice is not the loss. Jephthah saved his nation sacrificing his happiness; his daughter purified Jephthah's heart sacrificing her life. Life is sacrifice. Without sacrifice, life is non-sense. Not happiness, but sacrifice is the purpose of life. Sacrifice is the zenith of life. I believe that Jephthah's suffering was necessary to save his nation, and that his daughter's death was necessary to save Jephthah himself. Hallowed is the name of God. Thus God saved Israel by Jephthah's sacrifice, and saved Jephthah's heart by his daughter's sacrifice.

27 April

"Abraham believed God, and it was counted to him for righteousness." Now to the one who works, the reward is not reckoned of grace, but of debt. But to the one who believes on God of justifying the sinner, the faith is counted for righteousness.

Romans 4: 3–5

Believing

I believe God when I can do nothing. _Believing is the greatest and best of all doings. What shall we do, so that we might serve the works of God? Jesus answered: "This is the work of God, that you believe on Him whom He sent" *(John 6: 29)*. Believing is the greatest work, and all other works are its fruits. I turn away from the busy, soul-harassing Christianity of incessant agitations, revivals, reforms, reconstructions, and betterment of the world. Rather I find peace and living power in the primitive gospel of Jesus and his disciples, the gospel of quiet rest in God's works for us, and not in our fruitless works for Him.

28 April

I know that in me dwells no good. For to will is present with me, but how to perform that which is good I do not find. For I do not do the good that I will; but the evil which I do not will, that I do.

Romans 7: 18–19

Agony of Sin

The agony of sin is an ethical experience. Upon examining myself by conscientious intuition, upon finding myself inclined to prefer darkness against God, and upon searching for a savior who is able to rescue this sinner, I have finally encountered Christ, the healer of this painful conscience of mine. And I came to know that sin was not against human but against God. Consequently the One who relieved me of this agony of sins must be a God-head.

29 April

> When Jesus had looked round about on the Pharisees with anger, being grieved for the hardness of their hearts, he said to the man, "Stretch forth your hand." And he stretched it out; and his hand was restored whole as the other.
>
> Mark 3: 5

Holy Anger

A Christian is not easily provoked. He or she avoids committing sin of anger. But this does not imply he or she is free from anger. A Christian commits holy anger. Paul said "Who is offended, and I burn not?" (*2 Corinthians 11: 29*) The word "burn" here is considered to mean "feel holy anger." David said, "Do not I hate them, O Lord, that hate You?" (*Psalms 139: 21*) Here too, the holy anger of the faithful is vividly expressed. True love accompanies anger. Without anger, love is shallow, if not false. God often pours His anger upon his people, because he loves them so deeply and strongly. "For whom the Lord loves He chastises, and scourges every son and daughter whom he receives" (*Hebrews 12: 6*).

30 April

Independence

More than gold, More than honor, More than knowledge, More than life, O You Independence. O you kings, O you princes, O you bishops, O you doctors, You are tyrants. Alone with Truth, Alone with Conscience, Alone with God, Alone with Christ, I am free.

01   May

Because I live, you shall live also.

John 14: 19

Living Christ

The Christian from the beginning have believed in the activity of the Living Christ. This belief is neither superstition, nor tradition of the church. But it is the believer's living experience. Every Christian who led thorough-going life of faith, firmly believes in this encounter of life. A person becomes a Christian not because one came to understand the truth of Christianity, but because one met Christ, and owned Him as one's lord; or because one was found by Him, taken prisoner of Him, and called to be His servant. The true Christian is the one who has entered into immediate personal relationship with the Living Christ. On this point, Augustine, Luther, Calvin, Wesley, all agree. In Christianity, conversion is not simply understanding, but rather entrance into direct personal relationship with the savior. If Christ is not now living, there will be no conversion. A person is converted not because the one apprehended the doctrine, but because the one was introduced into the presence of Living Christ and one's whole life changed as the result of this encounter.

02 May

Those who sow in tears shall reap in joy. One who goes forth and weeps, bearing precious seed, shall doubtless come again with rejoicing, bringing one's grain.

Psalms 126: 5–6

Reward

God rewards us fully in other world, but also partially in this world. God gives us fruits of our labor and revives our fainting hope. God makes no disappointment for our labor of sowing the Gospel but give us hope of how wonderful will be the time of harvest. How joyful is to see the fruit of Spirit. When I see a true Christian as the fruit of my labor of blood and tears for ten or twenty years, my joy flows out as if my soul ascends to heaven. A fellow person discovered God, the Creator of the universe and human beings, and I was an instrument for that discovery. How joyful is to see that we could serve a person for the discovery of God.

03 May

Amaziah the priest of Bethel sent to Jeroboam king of Israel, saying, Amos has plotted against you in the midst of the house of Israel; the land is not able to bear all his words. For so Amos says; Jeroboam shall die by the sword, and Israel shall surely go into exile out of his land. Amaziah said to Amos ..., Prophesy not again any more at Bethel; for it is the king's chapel, and it is the king's court.

Amos 7: 10–13

Heresy

People scorn heresy. But nothing can be more precious than heresy in the world. Only with heresy can the world make progress. The prophet was a heretic. Jesus was a heretic. Paul also was a heretic. Luther was a heretic as well. Wesley, similarly, was a heretic. Because of their heresy they can still influence the world today. Heretics arise from their innermost conviction. It discerns truth without depending upon human authority. Heresy subjects itself directly to truth. It marches straight to truth and the God of truth without regarding humans. Heresy, thus, always keeps new life; the stereotyped should not be heresy. Heresy may have several errings, but it goes ahead persistently. If a person shuts heresy out, the one will face the risk of deadlock. The old shall invariably follow the orthodox faith; but the youths should not hesitate to be heresy.

04   May

The law of the LORD is perfect, converting the soul; the testimony of the LORD is sure, making wise the simple. The statutes of the LORD are right, rejoicing the heart; the commandment of the LORD is pure, enlightening the eyes. The fear of the LORD is clean, enduring for ever; the judgments of the LORD are true and righteous altogether. More to be desired are they than gold, yea, than much fine gold; sweeter also than honey and the honeycomb.

Psalms 19: 7–10

Value of Bible

Why is the Bible the word of God? Because it speaks what can be possible only by God. Unpolished or unskillfulness of its sentences is not the matter. Misrepresentations of historical facts or lacks of scientific evidence do not affect the importance of free revelation of God's will at all. We wish to know God's will about our life and our universe. And the Bible satisfies this wish most precisely. That is to say, the Bible is perfect, not because of its formality of words but because of God's holy will penetrating it throughout. Grace of God overflows the Bible; this is why the Bible is the word of God.

05   May

Do not labor for the food that perishes, but for that food which endures to everlasting life, which the Son of man will give you. For God the Father sealed Him.

John 6: 27

Faith and Labor

Faith cannot be maintained by faith as such. It is maintained only by labor. Faith is the root, and labor the branch. The former gives out the sap, while the latter assimilates it. Without branches and leaves, the sap will get rotten and petrified. Without labor, faith will degrade and bring forth skepticism. What is required for keeping faith shall not be more faith, but labor with the hand and brain. Without labor, the flesh starves and the soul perishes. Labor is indispensable not merely for sustaining the physical body alone but for the spirit.

06 May

I have learned to be content in whatever state I am. I know both how to be abased, and I know how to abound. In everything and in all things I am instructed both to be full and to be hungry, both to abound and to suffer need. I can do all things through Christ who strengthens me.

Philippians 4: 11–13

Dependence and Independence

A person of content shall be a person of independence. A discontented person is a person of dependence. This world is a fair place to live in for an independent person who relies on God alone. To a person who is depended on the favor of fellow humans, on the other hand, this world must be fooling one's own life; the one will get angry when denied their favor, and spend weary days ever complaining of the cold humanity. Happiness always rests on one's own hands and heart with God. Seeking it elsewhere as other's hands, the inevitable recompense will be disappointment, shame and discontent.

07   May

Do not know that your body is the temple of the Holy Spirit in you, whom you have of God? And you are not your own, for you are bought with a price. Therefore glorify God in your body and in your spirit, which are God's.

1 Corinthians 6: 19–20

Serve God

God abides not in The heavenly sphere of the Plough, the Orion and the Pleiades but among human beings. As Christopher said, "Human is the genuine temple of God." When thunderbolts shake mountains and troubles waters, this is not a time when God speaks to human. But God abides and speaks to us when and where a baby lay in us. God demands of us faith and obedience to Him. And to serve God is to serve humans. Without loving humans we have no way to serve God.

08 May

Let not your heart be troubled; you believe in God, believe also in me. In my Father's house are many mansions; if it were not so, I would have told you. I go to prepare a place for you. And if I go and prepare a place for you, I will come again, and receive you to myself; that where I am, there you may be also.

John 14: 1–3

Stranger in World

My life on earth may not be the matter; I maybe hated, misunderstood, poverty-stricken, or even naked. My eternal destiny is not determined by the circumstances surrounding me upon this earth. Jesus Christ, who gave up his life for me, is the One who determines my destiny. He went up to His Father to prepare a place for me. He promised to come back here again to receive us to Him. I am a stranger and a wanderer for a time in this world (*Psalms 119: 19*). I pitch a tent temporarily, and not building an eternal mansion, upon this earth. Whenever called by God, I will at once cut off the lope of the tent and hasten home into His Nation.

09 May

If you abide in Me, and My words abide in you, you shall ask what you will, and it shall be done to you. In this My Father is glorified, that you bear much fruit, so you shall be My disciples.

John 15: 7–8

Prayer for God's Will

A prayer that is surely heard is the prayer for the fulfillment of the will of God. By praying for His will, our prayer should never be a failure. One may then say, "If God's will is to be sorely accomplished, why has human to pray for it? God will do His will without human's prayer." Not so. God works with us to accomplish His will. God wants us to join for His work. Even the earthly father does not want to do his work, leaving his son isolated. It is the father's will to let the son participate in his work, and to share the glory with his son. Quite the same with the Heavenly Father. He wants to see that His own will reach Him through human prayer, and to accomplish it, so that human may partake of God's glory. So be that will of God of Love. So be the honor of mine to pray. Nothing more glorious for me than to pray for God's will as my own. When my will coincides with God's, and when my prayer coincides with God's design, nothing should then remain unfulfilled.

10 May

Our floor is green field. Our house is the trees of cedar and fir. Our gallery is the roses of Sharon and lilies of the valleys.

Song of Solomon 1: 16–18

My Church

My church is God's universe, the nature. Its roof is the blue sky, its rafters are the stars, its floor is the green fields and the colorful flowers, its musical instruments are the branches of pine trees, and its musicians are the little birds of the forest; its pulpit is the summit of the mountains, and the preacher is God himself. This is the church for non-church Christians. This church is far better than the Church of England or the Church of Rome. One who belongs no church eventually has the best church.

11 May

And out of the ground the LORD God formed every animal of the field and every fowl of the air, and brought them to Adam to see what he would call them. And whatever Adam called each living creature, that was its name.

Genesis 2: 19

Learn Natural History

God created human beings according to His image. Therefore human can understand the will of God. One of the purposes that God created the earth is to make it serve for the development of human understanding. It is our duty to learn His creatures and the earth and to develop our understanding. In the beginning God created animals of the field and birds of the air and brought them to Adam to learn them. Thus the study of natural history is God's first revelation to human understanding. Learn God's creatures through His direct instruction. This is a way to know God and a method to study the truth. Natural history is the first science of human beings. Adam learned to distinguish animals and to classify birds. How blessed is to study natural history. There is no harm, but much reward. We can reach God through the Nature. Come fellows, listen to the song of birds in the mountain and learn the life of wild animals in the field.

12 May

The LORD is my Shepherd; I shall not want. He makes me to lie down in green pastures; He leads me beside the still waters. He restores my soul; He leads me in paths of righteousness for His name's sake. Yea, though I walk through the valley of the shadow of death, I will fear no evil; for You are with me; Your rod and Your staff, they comfort me. You prepare a table for me in the presence of my enemies; You anoint my head with oil; my cup runs over. Surely goodness and mercy shall follow me all the days of my life; and I shall dwell in the house of the LORD forever.

Psalms 23: 1–6

Lord, My Shepherd

I owe to Jehovah what I am today. I tried to abandon Jehovah; but He did not allow me to leave. I tried to become a man of this world; but He drove me into His Nation by crushing my desires. Jehovah leads me with His staff and rod; He leads me today to lie down in green pastures and beside the still waters. Steep and harsh was my life in the past; but this worked good for me. I rushed to God to be healed. Like a foolish sheep, I was driven into the Lord's pastures.

13 May

And now, says the LORD who formed me from the womb to be His servant, to bring Jacob again to Him, Though Israel is not gathered, yet I shall be glorious in the eyes of the LORD, and my God shall be my strength. And He said, "It is but a little thing that you should be My servant to raise up the tribes of Jacob, and to bring back the preserved ones of Israel; I will also give you for a light to the nations, to be My salvation to the end of the earth."

Isaiah 49: 5–6

Servant of God

Humans have no power to carry out the work of God no matter how they make effort. God alone carries out His work, and a servant of God is to obey His commandments. The servant of God can speak and work only according to His voice. God fulfills His work by Himself, and the servant is mere an instrument for His work. Exodus was not the work of Moses and Aaron, who were mere messengers to speak the commandment of God in front of Pharaoh, the king of Egypt. God himself stretched His almighty hands and saved His chosen people. Isaiah, Paul and all other servants as well, acted only according to the command of God. Therefore they could fulfilled the great work. A servant of God has no own plan of work, but just speaks and works of God. The servant has to declare the commandment of God without being afraid of the face of humans and work despite of scorn and mocking of the people. The great plan of God is fulfilled beyond the intention of the servant. What God requires to a servant is not one's wisdom and power, but faith and courage. The servant is a tool of God to fulfill His great work.

14   May

Prophesy to these bones, and say to them, O dry bones, hear the word of the LORD. So says the Lord to these bones; Behold, I will cause breath to enter into you, and you shall live. And I will lay pillars on you, and will bring up flesh on you, and cover you with skin, and put breath in you, and you shall live. And you shall know that I am the LORD. So I prophesied as I was commanded. And as I prophesied, there was a noise. And behold, a shaking. And the bones came near, a bone to its bone.

Ezekiel 37: 4–7

Hope of Resurrection

"Rachel weeping for her children, would not be comforted" (*Jeremiah 31: 15*). But there is one way to be comforted. If somehow my beloved live again; if by some power the one whose eyes and lips have been closed can be revived to stand before me, talk with me, receive my love and return the same love to me; in a word, if the one could be resurrected, truly I will be comforted and my lament will be healed perfectly. People may laugh at hearing "resurrection," but it is the very desire longed by everybody who suffers from separation by death. We cannot bear eternal separation. Without, death is a "great mourning that would not be comforted," if the hope of resurrection and reunion were in vain.

15 May

Divisions are necessary among you, to be seen clearly which of you have God's approval.

1 Corinthians 11: 19

Differences in Faith

Differences in faith may be unavoidable; but the judgment of other's faith must be avoided by all means. While rejecting the Catholic, the Episcopal and the Methodist faith, I have to express my deepest respect for their earnestness. To achieve discernment, a clear distinction is essential. People know I am not a Buddhist but a Christian, not a Roman Catholic but a Protestant, and not a church-follower but a non-church follower. By this distinct difference, let people hate me if they will. To be loved by opponents should be more unfortunate than being hated by friends. Clear distinction of belief is indispensable for faith.

16 May

Peter came to Jesus and said, Lord, how often shall my brother sin against me and I forgive him? Until seven times? Jesus said to him, I do not say to you, Until seven times; but, Until seventy times seven.

Matthew 18: 21–22

Forgive Seventy Times Seven

Jesus forgave his enemies. He benevolently pardoned them seventy times seven. His follower should not conceive enmity or make resentment in heart. We ought to forgive, with the love of Christ, all who sinned against us. If righteous Christ forgave those who nailed Him to the cross, why not we, sinful beings, follow the same? Gladly are we to forgive enemies, how painfully their insult may vex us. If we cannot forgive enemies, we are not Christians, even if we profess to know God's presence. If we cannot renounce resentment in heart, we are not Christians, however possessed with deep knowledge of Christianity and complete understanding of the dogma. God bears long-suffering; and Christianity teaches a religion of long-suffering. A Christian can pardon all offences committed against him or her.

17 May

For God so loved the world that He gave His only-begotten Son, that whoever believes in Him should not perish but have everlasting life.

John 3: 16

God's Love and Human's Faith

The greatest thing in God is His Love. The greatest thing in human is faith in God. In God's love and human's responding faith is there reconciliation: God's joy and human's salvation. Love and Faith are the two greatest things in the world. Theology that does not come up to these two, the church that does not cling to these two, and Christian mission that is not conducted upon these two, are no worth here or anywhere.

18 May

Continue in prayer, and watch in the same with thanksgiving.

Colossians 4: 2

Prayer of Thanksgiving

The major portion of my prayer is not wishing. I start my prayer with wholehearted thanks. I thank my God for having prepared such a wonderful universe to live in. My deepest thanks are for being granted with good friends, with works to devote my life to, with a heart to discern good from evil and look up to God of righteousness. I thank especially for the unfathomable depth of the mercy of God; when I was preoccupied by selfish gains and lusts, far away from God, He saved my soul and corrected my way by the revelation of Jesus Christ. Then my heart overflows with gratefulness I say, "Thanks" to the bunch of little violets on the wayside. Also I am grateful for the gentle breeze that strokes my cheeks. Or rising early in the morning, and viewing the infiltrating golden glory in the eastern sky, I psalms of thanksgiving.

19 May

Ask and it shall be given to you; seek and you shall find; knock and it shall be opened to you. For each one who asks receives; and one who seeks finds; and to one who knocks, it shall be opened.

Matthew 7: 7–8

Seek Truth

Religion seeks the truth as such; it is the great power of religion to constribute science. Truth is holy; no one can reach the depth of the truth without a sincere heart. Truth is like an intimate friend. Meet her with humble heart; then she will gladly open and show her chest of treasure. She never shows herself where one is driven by pride, deep in jealousy and merely seeking fame and selfish gains. Self-interest clouds one's eyes of observation and deprives one's key to open the hidden door of truth. There is no progress of science without true religion. Decline of science comes from where true religion is faded. The great discovery in science arises in the nation where the people respect religion. Ponder truth deeply.

20   May

For You shall be a witness for Jesus Christ to all humans of what you have seen and heard.

Acts 22: 15

Witnessing

Christianity is essentially witnessing. It is neither reasoning nor even preaching in modern sense of the term. *Kerusso* in New Testament Greek is more witnessing than preaching; it is proclaiming, announcing, making known what we have seen and experienced. We can do this witnessing to anybody, regardless whether one accepts it or not. And the Christian is duty-bound to make such witnessing, as was the man born blind said to his inquisitors: "Whether he (Jesus) be a sinner, I know not; one thing I know, that, whereas I was blind, now I see." *(John 9: 25)* The same we can say; we cannot preach or reason; but "one thing, I know, that, whereas I was blind, now I see."

21 May

Cain brought to the LORD an offering of the fruit of the ground. And Abel also brought of the firstlings of his flock and of the fat of it. And the LORD had pleased to Abel and to his offering, but He did not have pleased to Cain and to his offering. And Cain glowed with anger, and his face fell.

Genesis 4: 3–5

Abel and Cain

Something must be sacrificed to God. But greatest care must be taken in selecting what to sacrifice. "The sacrifices of God are a broken spirit" (*Psalms 51: 17*). So the sacrifices must represent this spirit. A broken spirit, a heart that find nothing good of one's own self but cries "O wretched man that I am. Who shall deliver me from the body of this death?" (*Romans 7: 24*). This heart is best represented by a lamb. The attitude of throwing oneself before the burning fire of righteousness to ask pardon is most vividly symbolized by the sacrifice of the first born lamb. Abel had this heart, but Cain did not. What Cain had were a sense of duty, responsibility and service. These were valuable senses, but not the most. God saw in Abel a heart to empty himself, and in Cain a heart that would not seek righteousness beyond his own. Thus God approved of Abel but not of Cain.

22 May

When the perfect thing comes, then that which is in part will be caused to cease.

1 Corinthians 13: 10

Perfection of Work in Heaven

The true work begins when we enter heaven. We are coworkers with God already in this life; and in the life to come, we enter into closer fellowship with Him in His creation-works. We hope for the perfection of our work in the life to come, which is the height of bliss. We are like Michelangelo standing with a chisel before his sculpture, or Leonardo da Vinci sitting with a brush before his canvas. True bliss is found only in action; life is action; and where there is no action, there is no life and no bliss. Heaven cannot be otherwise than constant, fruitful, perfect and blessing actions. And we are destined for such a life, and such an action. Oh, bliss it is to have been born, and also to have suffered and still to suffer.

23 May

This is the work of God that you believe on Christ whom he has sent.

John 6: 29

Belief as Work

The essence of true Christianity is neither to work nor to attempt to work; it is simply to believe. I believe that God loves me not because I am good but because I am His creature, His child. I believe that He loves me with His fatherly love, and helps me more than I ask. Such a belief on my part prepares me to receive strength in my inmost being ethically, psychologically, and even physically, which comes from the infinite depth of His Being. Without my attempting to work, I am made to work by the power which works in me; I simply believe in Him. And He works mightily in and through me ... All this is a matter of practical experience. I need no dogma to support me in my belief; no bishop to confirm me in it. Any person can believe if he or she wills to believe. Only it takes courage to believe. Indeed, to believe is the greatest deed of humankind.

24 May

We know that we have passed from death to life, because we love the brothers. He who does not love his brother abides in death. Everyone hating one's brother is a murderer. And you know that no murderer has everlasting life abiding in.

1 John 4: 14–15

Christianity is Love

Christianity is neither church nor dogma. It is love; not love in general, but love in specific. Christianity is primarily and essentially love of enemies. God so loved the world, the rebellious, apostate, God-hating world, that He gave His only begotten son. That is Christianity. Then, how about those so-called Christian nations with all their churches, doctrines, theologies, bishops, doctors of divinities, foreign missionaries and social services, yet intensely hating their enemies who are mostly "brother-Christians," declaring war against one another, and delighting over the fall of their rivals, and preparing for another and next war? Without free, generous, joyful love of enemies, there is no Christianity to speak about.

25 May

For we do not wrestle against flesh and blood, but against principalities, against powers, against the world's rulers, of the darkness of this age, against spiritual wickedness in high places. Therefore take to yourselves the whole armor of God, that you may be able to withstand in the evil day, and having done all, to stand.

Ephesians 6: 12–13

Battle against Satan

We can not avoid battle at all as long as we stand for the Gospel of Christ in this world. We fight neither to make others suffer nor to get our revenge. We, of course, love peace most. We wish to spend our life in studying the Bible and in fellowship with God, His children and His Creatures. But the Lord does not allow us to do so, who saved us from sin by sacrificing himself on the battle of the Cross. We also have to struggle against Satan, who is wickedness of spirit "within" and also of flesh "without." He reveals himself as hypocrites, deceiver, drunkards, bribers, adulterers, cruel persons and the like. We sometimes have to condemn them, not being afraid of their anger.

26 May

There is therefore now no condemnation to them which are in Christ Jesus, who walk not after the flesh, but after the Spirit. For the law of the Spirit of life in Christ Jesus has made me free from the law of sin and death... . For they that are after the flesh do mind the things of the flesh; but they that are after the Spirit the things of the Spirit.

Romans 8: 1–2, 4

Spirit and Flesh

Christianity is neither stoicism nor of course its opposite licentiousness. It is a living way to replace a life of flesh with of spirit. It teaches us not to abide in flesh, not to be governed by flesh and not to let flesh predominate over us. Rather, it gives us the power of spirit to control the flesh. Paul therefore says, "but if you through the Spirit do mortify the deeds of the flesh, you shall live" (*Romans 8: 13*). He never says "by self-mortification" but "through the Spirit." This is a clear way in measuring, and definite in effect. It well answers common sense, bearing fruit everlasting. By faith, to look up to Jesus, to be granted with the reward of the Holy Spirit, and to walk according to its guidance. By doing this, the flesh shall be rightly controlled without turning to the extremes of either stoicism or licentiousness.

27 May

Abraham puzzled not at the promise of God through unbelief; but was firm in faith, giving glory to God.

Romans 4: 20

Belief

Belief is neither an intellectual act nor a result of careful investigations. It is rather an apprehension of truth with one's whole being. Belief is therefore spontaneous. Psychologically, it is an act akin to one's falling in love with a person; one sees and believes the person. The relationship between God and the faithful is intimate like this; God speaks, and a faithful trusts in His words. God calls, and a faithful responds by saying: "Here I am; send me" (*Isaiah 6: 8*). We cannot make a person a belief with all our arguments. All we can do is to witness our beliefs. Belief is sweet perception; it is human's falling in love with God and His truth.

28 May

Well done, good and faithful servant; You have been faithful over a few things, I will make you ruler over many things; enter into the joy of your lord.

Matthew 25: 23

True Love of Nation

To be loyal to one's country, one does not need take up politics or military. To serve society, one does not need do social work. Nothing is more patriotic and public serving than doing one's own calling faithfully, according to one's own faculty. Rembrandt painted pictures and honored the name of Holland. Wordsworth wrote poetry and changed the social morals of the British people. The way of public service is not limited to one. Any calling when done faithfully, is a work that enriches a country and purifies a nation. Not necessarily on a platform at parliament, but within a solitarily study, one can fully influence generations to come. Not necessarily engaged in a charity work, but secluded lecturing on the Bible, one can perform a greater love than the charity work. Do faithfully what you are sent to this world for, and you can contribute to your country, transform your society and, yea, you can even move the whole universe. Pray, and be quiet. Give up "movement" or "propaganda," and be a little but great patriot, or a reformer.

29 May

Paul called the disciples to continue in the faith and preached that through much suffering we must enter into the Nation of God.

Acts 14: 22

Need of Suffering

Suffering is a necessary condition of life. A person come to God though suffering. By suffering one dies in flesh, lives in spirit, and enters everlasting life. This is why suffering lasts throughout life. The world without suffering is the world unbearable in deed. Everlasting life is to know God. We come to know God and enter everlasting life when we share suffering with His son. Do not escape suffering, but endure and overcome it. I believe that suffering is the way of the Gospel of Christ.

30　May

Truly I say to you, unless you are converted and become as little children, you shall not enter into the Nation of Heaven.

Matthew 18: 3

Simple Christianity

Christianity, we understand, is very simple. We might almost say, it is simplicity itself. Negatively, Christianity is not morality, not social reforms, not "ethical evangelism," not "international ethics," and not any other of modern "isms." But Christianity is God's grace and human's appreciation by faith. Grace and Faith are the kernel of Christianity. It is simple enough to understood even by a child. Indeed, only children can understand it. A year, a month, a day, an hour, yes even a moment is enough to understand Grace and Faith.

31 May

It is the spirit that makes alive; the flesh profits nothing; the words that I speak to you are spirit and are life.

John 6: 63

Spiritual Christianity

Christianity is spiritual. Christ is the savior of our spirit... We, Christians, dies in flesh and lives in spirit; we neither pursue the success in this world nor seek the fame of people. Rather we seeks the ideal unceasingly, keeps the hope of the youth to the end, rejoice in suffering, lives as a prophet not as a churchgoer. To be a spiritual Christian, be alert of the success of this world. Seek the higher ideal when you have a worldly success. Break out of the stereotype and formality of life. Be militant spiritually against this world and its power. Life is everlasting, not fossilized. Life resists this world and is not overcome. May we be young forever spiritually as a child of God.

01 June

We suffer with Christ, that we may be also glorified together. For I reckon that the sufferings of this present time are not worthy to be compared with the glory which shall be revealed in us.

Romans 8: 17–18

Problem of Life

All people suffer from life, and it is the greatest problem of life. But, once the power of God is poured forth, the question of suffering, totally incomprehensible as it is, will instantly be dissolved. Many a person who encounters with Christianity and studies the Bible, faces a keen tension with the problem of life. All the problem, however, shall melt away if and when God's Holy Spirit is received, leaving behind the unspeakable gratefulness alone. You therefore pray for the advent of the Holy Spirit. It, however, can be attained only by step by step. Thus, we are to aim at an everlasting advance from knowledge to knowledge, from faith to faith.

02   June

Is not this the carpenter's son? Is not his mother called Mary? And his brothers, James and Joses and Simon and Judas, and his sisters, are they not all with us? Then from where does this man have all these things?

Matthew 13: 55–56

Jesus without Titles

Jesus was not the Pope, nor the bishop, nor the pastor, nor the missionary, nor the doctors. He did not put a crown on his head nor embellished garments around his body. He was, in fact, never a man of the clergy. He never received a salary for his faith. He was simply a plain man of Nazareth, engaged in his father's occupation, carpentry. Thus he knew God intuitively, not by accumulating religious knowledge at the theological school or an institute of philosophy. I adore him because he was a great plain man.

03   June

The Lord Jehovah will do nothing unless He reveals His secret to His servants the prophets. The lion has roared; who will not fear? The Lord Jehovah has spoken; who will not prophesy?

Amos 3: 7–8

Truth and Prophecy

Whoever speaks the truth is a prophet. There is no understanding of the truth without prophecy. To true humanity, prophecy is a necessary condition. Prophecy is a warning not to bypass the judgment, but to realize the judgment of God when it takes place and to repent and be saved. Without prophecy, a judgment is regarded as a mere disaster and not recognized as the righteous will of God. In that case, the judgment will become a bothering event and not lead to repentance for salvation. Blessed is the nation which has a prophet.

04 June

We ourselves also were once foolish, disobedient, deceived, slaving for various lusts and pleasures, living in malice and envy, hateful, disputing one another. But when the kindness and love of God our Savior toward human appeared, not by works of righteousness which we have done, but according to His mercy He saved us, through the washing of rebirth and renewal of the Holy Spirit, whom He poured out on us abundantly through Jesus Christ our Savior.

Titus 3: 3–6

Mercy of Salvation

I was saved against my will. I loved this world, but God crushed all my worldly attempts and compelled me to look nowhere but to the world to come. I craved for human love, but God sent me many opponents to break my illusion about humankind and forced me to rely on the Father in Heaven. If my life had been as I desired, I would certainly be spending now a common human life without God and the world to come. I was compelled by God to come to His salvation. So, on my own part, nothing merits my salvation.

05 June

The time is fulfilled, and the Nation of God is at hand. Repent and believe the gospel.

Mark 1: 15

Repentance

"Repentance" has a deep meaning in the New Testament. It is not to regret sin and amend it. The original word "metanoia" means "transforming the heart and mind." This implies to change the purpose of life, which errors completely without knowing true God, the Father of Christ. Jesus teaches us not merely to renew our heart but to transform our "mind," the view of the world. From this we come to know that "repentance" is not only of sentiment but also of intellect. It means transformation of inner eyes toward the whole creation. "Believe the gospel." Believe the words that reveals the heart of God. See the whole creation as God looks upon it. Unite your heart and mind with Him.

06 June

You shall not eat of flesh with the life in it, or the blood of it.

Genesis 9: 4

Food and Character

When our Lord said: "Not that which goes into the mouth defiles a person; but that which comes out of the mouth, this defiles a person" (*Matthew 15: 11*), He stated a religious principle, not physiological or moral effect. Physiologically, that which goes into the mouth does defile a human, and when it continued as a habit, defiles moral. That is to say, one's food does affect one's character. A meat-eater becomes carnivorous, and a vegetable-eater becomes sheep-like. Beefsteak-fed men and women can never be expected to be the meek followers of the Prince of Peace. Their passionateness, aggressiveness, and boundless ambition for world-domination, testify to the strong animal nature of their food.

07   June

I am the vine, you are the branches. One who abides in Me, and I in him or her, the same brings forth much fruit; for without Me you can do nothing.

John 15: 5

Act with Prayer

A person of prayer is not a person who just professes prayer. The person does things with prayer. Or better, the person cannot do anything unless with prayer. The person studies with prayer, works with prayer, or struggles with prayer. In fact, the person does everything in and by the power of God, instead of one's own.

08 June

Come to me, all you that labor and are heavy laden, and I will give you rest. Take my yoke upon you, and learn of me; for I am meek and lowly in heart; and you shall find rest to your souls. For my yoke is easy, and my burden is light.

Matthew 11: 28–30

Life of Christian

Don't upset hardships of life. Faith in God will make your life the easiest to live. When I leave myself entirely to my God, my duties will be done by myself, my deserting friends will leave without compelling, my bound friends will come without asking, my corruptions will vanish in due time, and my portions will come to me without demanding. A Christian's life is effortless way. He or she simply goes to God. Then God will care for all one's needs. Blessed be the Father, my God.

09 June

Behold, the days come, says the LORD, that I will make a new covenant with the house of Israel, and with the house of Judah... I will put My law in their inward parts, and write it in their hearts; and I will be their God, and they shall be My people. And they shall no more teach their neighbor and their brother, saying, Know the LORD; for they shall all know me, from the least of them to the greatest of them, says the LORD. For I will forgive their iniquity, and I will remember their sins no more.

Jeremiah 31: 31, 33–34

New Bible

The Bible is great. But living Christ is greater than the Bible. We miss the essence if we do not touch Him by studying the Bible. The Bible records Christ's activities in the past. We ought to make the Bible anew by receiving His spirit to-day. Nobody can truly understand the Bible without making a new Bible from the old Bible. The Bible has yet to be completed. And we are to add the materials to its last pages.

10 June

Thus says God the LORD, He who created the heavens and stretched them out, spreading out the earth and its offspring; He who gives breath to the people on it and spirit to those who walk in it.

Isaiah 42: 5

God of Universe and Human

I return to the old, afar monotheism conceived by Moses, Isaiah, Jeremiah, Jesus, Paul and others. It is the God who, in the beginning, created the heaven, the earth and all the creatures therein. There is also the God "Immanuel" who abides with human beings. Both are not two Gods, but are one same God, who created the universe, presides over it, and descends to its midst to sustain it. This is not the god of deism, who stands high, aloof from the process of the universe and human life, touching nothing and sensing nothing. Nor is it the god confined within the universe and incapable of doing anything beyond what pertains to nature. God created the universe but is greater than it. He gradually reveals Himself through the universe. His will shall be the way of human beings. One can know about God through the universe, but His will can only be known by direct approach to Him.

11 June

The Jews' Passover was at hand, and Jesus went up to Jerusalem, And found in the temple those that sold oxen and sheep and doves, and the changers of money sitting; And when he had made a scourge of small cords, he drove them all out of the temple, and the sheep, and the oxen; and poured out the changers' money, and overthrew the tables; And said to them that sold doves, Take these things hence; make not my Father's house an house of merchandise.

John 2: 13–16

Accusation of Sin

God is Love and, at the same time, a Burning Fire. God does not tolerate evil: "He will not at all acquit the wicked" (*Nahum 1: 3*). God graciously pardons human sins, but this is not "unconditional." All who believe in Christ will be graciously pardoned by the righteousness of faith. But God judges our sins. We take refugee the Cross of Christ for our sinfulness. The Cross, indeed, is the culmination of the punishment of our sins.

12 June

I tell the truth in Christ, I do not lie, my conscience also bearing me witness in the Holy Spirit, that I have great heaviness and continual sorrow in my heart. For I could wish that myself were accursed from Christ for my brothers, my country-people according to the flesh who are Israelites.

Romans 9: 1–4

Two-centered Faith

Religion is neither just private nor just public. It should begin with private but end to public. Perfect faith is not one-centered circle, but two-centered ellipse. Faith centers in oneself and others. It starts from oneself, but not self-satisfied; it further has to center others. One's salvation by Christ sympathizes the salvation of others and of the world. For the first time we come to realize the deep meaning of the salvation of Christ when we go to public.

13   June

Those on the good ground are the ones who, in an honest and good heart, having heard the Word, keep it and bring forth fruit with patience.

Luke 8: 15

Keep Faith

In the nation of disbelievers, it is a great challenge to keep faith. A faithful needs not to build a church, or to gather many believers, or to write a great religious book. Just keep faith bravely, firmly to the end. But it is very difficult to keep the Gospel pure among disbelievers. The fact tells us that thousands of once believers forsake the faith and millions left the faith. It is especially the most difficult to keep faith without depending on the churches, the missionaries or other's aids. Let us thank God for the great miracle that He kept our faith pure. For thirty, forty or fifty, I was allowed to speak the gospel and to keep my faith in midst of oppositions, neglects, and despises by the society. Just keep faith firmly within and independently without worrying of the life. This is the mission.

14 June

For even the Son of man came not to be served to, but to serve, and to give his life a ransom for many.

Mark 10: 45

Serving to Human

Salvation means serving humans, that is, doing good to others, laboring for others, and, in fact, giving oneself to others. If a brother suffers from debts, let it not be passed by as a matter of no concern but let everything be willingly done to save him from the bondage of debts. And sin is the greatest debt of ours; so, God willed that this heaviest debt should be removed from humanity in and by Christ. This heart is pleased by God, and therewith Christ is called by the name of God. The same heart, to some extent, is cherished even by us whose humanity is deeply involved in sin. How much more by God Himself. For the sake of the name of God, He must as well be a Redeemer. He will infallibly and voluntarily bear human debt and to remove its sting from humanity. Christ came into this world with this heart of God. By Christ we know that God never betrays our hope and is truly our Redeemer.

15 June

Astounding and horrible thing is committed in the land; The prophets prophesy falsely, and the priests bear rule by their means; and my people love to have it so; and what will you do in the end thereof?

Jeremiah 5: 30–31

Need of Reformation

The world needs reformation of the Christian Religion again. The Reformation of the 16th century ended as an interrupted movement. Protestantism has been institutionalized and returned back to the discarded Roman Catholicism. We need another reformation to bring Protestantism to its ideal consequences. The new Protestantism must be perfectly free from a trace of churchism; it must be a fellowship, not an institution; it is free communion of souls, not a system or an organization. Practically, it will be churchless Christianity, calling no person bishop or pastor, save Jesus Christ. Does God intend Japan to be the country where such Christianity is to appear, the new experiment to be tried in the religious history of humankind, to begin Christianity anew in the Land of the Rising Sun?

16 June

The fruit of the Spirit is in all goodness and righteousness and truth.

Ephesians 5: 9

Best Grace

It is a grievous misconception to see the grace of God in the happiness and success of life. Such misconception leads us to doubt and loses the faith in God. The best grace of God that is given to us is the Holy Spirit, not happiness. The Holy Spirit creates us goodness, the heart of love to God and people, the heart of thank at any circumstances, and the peace of mind. This grace comes immediately though the Holy Spirit, and has nothing to do with the happiness and success of worldly life. Rather in many cases, the grace is opposite to the happiness and success. We do not care whether we have the happiness or not. The essential thing that we need is goodness. That's all, and nothing more. The goal of life is to pursue the heart of goodness.

17 June

The LORD hears when I call to Him. Stand in awe, and sin not; commune with your own heart on your bed and be still. Offer the sacrifices of righteousness, and trust in the LORD... You have put gladness in my heart, more than in the time that their grain and their wine increased. I will lie down, both in peace and in sleep. For You alone, LORD, make me dwell in safety.

Psalms 4: 3–8

Independence and Unity

Independence is not isolation. Independence means to stand alone with God, while isolation means having none else to stand with. An individual can stand with God; and the one can become God's friend. Anyone who says, "Independence brings about isolation" has not yet tried seriously to be independent. Independence can hardly be isolated. No one else, in reality, can have more companions than an independent one. As Carlyle said: "the unity of humankind can only be achieved when each individual has attained independence." An independent one loves same independent persons. Where independent persons are united together, there will be the most unified community, although it is based on the independent mind to stand alone. Here arises a paradox of life; there is the most unified community is realized where uniformity is not called for.

18   June

Who shall separate us from the love of Christ? Shall tribulation, or distress, or persecution, or famine, or nakedness, or peril, or sword? As it is written, "For Your sake we are killed all the day long. We are counted as sheep of slaughter." But in all these things we more than conquer through Him who loved us. For I am convinced that neither death, nor life, nor angels, nor principalities, nor powers, nor things present, nor things to come, nor height, nor depth, nor any other creature, shall be able to separate us from the love of God which is in Christ Jesus our Lord.

Romans 8: 35–39

Victory of Love

Jesus is the only person who did not commit sin by any means. He is the person who was not angered by crowning with thorns, buffeting with fists, spitting on the face, or by nailing on the cross. Let the tempest of enmity rage as it will, yet the rock of love could not be moved. Though the tide of hated press on as it will, the shore of love could not be beaten. Christ's death means love's victory over hatred. Here, hatred, with its fierce bolt, clashed against love, and was defeated. From now on, hatred cannot boast its malice. Once overcome by the Son of Man, its destruction has already been sentenced. Christ's death in love disclosed a direction to world peace. Christ was raised on the cross, to raise love to the highest Throne.

19 June

But if we died with Christ, we believe that we shall also live with Him.

Romans 6: 8

Christ Within Me

Christ now in heaven on the right hand of the Father, leaves me not desolate. He dwells in me by His Spirit, and leads me, teaches me, and comforts me, as when He was with His disciples in the days of His flesh. The Christian is strong, not because of one's incomparable faith, but because of the strong Son of God who works through he Christian. I am more than a conqueror through Him, that is, through the Spirit of Christ who is with me. Christ is a present reality within me, not merely a past or future thing, but a working power now and here.

20 June

Jesus saw Nathanael coming to Him and said of him, Behold an Israelite indeed in whom is no guile... . Nathanael said to Him, Rabbi, You are the Son of God. You are the King of Israel.

John 1: 47, 49

To Be A Christian

A doctor asked me: "What is to be a Christian?" I answered him: "To be a Christian is to trust in God, and to deliver all things to Him, your sins and transgressions included. It is to do to God as your patient would trust in you and leave one's sick body entirely in your care. No more and no less. It is not necessary to join any particular church, to pass through any set of ceremonies, to sign any form of doctrines. Faith in God, the Heavenly Father, is the sole thing needed, and all other good things follow as its consequences. The doctor said: "Then I too can be a Christian." I said: "You are the one, right now."

21 June

Woe to you, scholars and Pharisees, hypocrites. For you cleanse the outside of the cup and of the dish, but inside you are full of extortion and excess.

Matthew 23: 25

Formalism

Externalism is dear to the human heart. It may take the form of culture and morality, or of "services," sacraments and churchly order, or of orthodoxy and philanthropy... Formalism can spring up and flourish on the most evangelical soil, and in the most strictly Pauline Churches. It is impossible to banne and barred out it completely, since it knows how to find entrance even under the simplest modes of worship and the soundest doctrine. The saw-toothed defense of Articles and Confessions can not prevent from its entry, and may even prove its cover and entrenchment. As the Apostle says, Only a constant "new creation" can overcome externalism and formalism (*Galatians 6: 15*).

22 June

Crying again with a loud voice, Jesus released His spirit. And, behold. The veil of the temple was torn in two from top to bottom. And the earth quaked, and the rocks were sheared, and the tombs were opened, and many bodies of the saints who had fallen asleep arose, and coming out of the tomb after His resurrection they went into the holy city and appeared to many. But the centurion and those guarding Jesus, seeing the earthquake, and the things that took place, they feared greatly, saying, Truly this One was Son of God.

Matthew 27: 50–54

Solemnity of Death

Death of a person is solemn. It embodies something supernatural and mystic. At the deathbed, one cannot be a mere animal, nor merely an intellectual organism. One has to face spiritual confrontation with one's death seriously. At one's death, one longs a world of eternity. One intuitively knows one cannot die through natural death. Nothing can be compared to human death for solemnity and awfulness. Standing by the deathbed of our beloved, we are like facing God in the heavenly Nation. This is for more than the saying: "With his last breath, one gives out the best of one's own." The scene is sacred. Where the last of human breath is drawn, there abides God with His host of angels. Empty-headed as the earthly life may be, it unfailingly has one moment, when death visits, of absolute solemnity and of sacredness.

23   June

Cast your burden upon the LORD, and he shall sustain you; he shall never suffer the righteous to be annoyed.

Psalms 55: 22

Righteous Person

"Cast your burden upon the Lord" and suffer not yourself to bear it. If you carry it by yourself, you will suffer intolerable afflictions. Put it on Jehovah, who can not just bear your burden on your behalf, but also give you peace of mind. He will never allow His righteous elect to be annoyed. The so-called "righteous" of the world may be swung, but the righteous of God, the one who depends upon Him, and stands in righteous relation with Him is never swung. The righteous of God is a person of faith, a person of trust, a person who draws righteousness from God, and never a person who proclaims "I am righteous," but the one who clings to God's mercy, crying "Pity this head of sinners." And never will such a person of righteousness be annoyed.

24 June

O human, what is good, and what does the LORD require of you? Is it to do justice and to love mercy and to walk humbly with your God?

Micah 6: 8

What is Religion

Religion is not temple, church, monastery, ritual, scripture, and even the Bible. It is everlasting life, or to live in everlasting life. There is no religion without everlasting life. The mission of religion, therefore, is not mere preaching, propagation, social reform, national welfare, baptism, or Lord Supper, but to give birth the new life of everlasting spirit and to care its growth. Thus religion has a specific object and clear goal as politics, economy or medicine does. In other worlds religion is not the art of self-satisfaction and consolation with music and eloquence, or vain talk of visionary, but the earnest labor to provide for practical needs of souls.

25 June

God has sent forth the Spirit of His Son into your hearts, crying, Abba, Father. So that you are no longer a slave, but a son; and if a son, also an heir of God through Christ.

Galatians 4: 6–7

Grace of Christ

I am saved by the righteous work done by Christ on my behalf. This is why I can approach God courageously in spite of unworthy myself. Howsoever, I shall ask His mercy not for my own sake, but for Christ's sake. I can then confidently approach on to God's throne, crying "Abba Father," even though unworthy as I am. I have no merit to ask anything for myself, but, I can ask all things of my Father for the sake of Jesus Christ.

26 June

Instruction must be by instruction, precept by precept; line by line, letter by letter; here a little, there a little

Isaiah 28: 10

Little by Little

Pouring the Holy Spirit is the work of God over our whole life. God pours us the Holy Spirit little by little. We, impure and sinful beings, cannot receive the Holy Spirit at once. "First the blade, then the ear, after that the full grain in the ear" (*Mark 4: 28*). Good receiving the Holy Spirit is gradual descendent. We hope that the Holy Spirit will not come violently like storm and thunder, but come silently like soft wind and due drop. We hope not to come drastic change in our life, except emergency.

27 June

He has borne our griefs, and carried our sorrows; but we thought that He was stricken, smitten by God, and afflicted. But He was wounded for our transgressions; He was bruised for our iniquities; the chastisement of our peace was on Him; and with His stripes we ourselves are healed.

Isaiah 53: 4–5

Servant of Suffering

The greatest thing is, not to conquer human but to be conquered by human. Resign your job if others demand; stand below others; suffer gladly other's insult; be spat and nailed to the cross. Thus done, and thus treated only, we can comprehend God's will. Alas, the high is lowered, and the low is heightened. Would you be heightened by God? Be first kicked bottommost by human.

28 June

In Jesus Christ you also trusted, after that you heard the word of truth, the gospel of your salvation, in whom also after that you believed, you were sealed with that holy Spirit of promise, Which is the earnest of our inheritance until the redemption of the purchased possession, to the praise of his glory.

Ephesians 1: 13–14

Trust in Jesus

I do not know whether I am a good man or a bad man;
I simply trust in Jesus.
I do not know whether I am doing good or evil;
I simply trust in Jesus.
I do not know whether I will enter heaven or fall into hell;
I simply trust in Jesus.
I trust in Jesus, yes, I trust in Jesus.
Whether I shall be lifted up to the height of heaven,
or be cast down to the depth of hell,
I shall ever trust in Jesus.

29 June

The path of the just is as the shining light, that shines more and more to the perfect day.

Proverbs 4: 18

Road of Righteous Person

Suppose one starts the least but ends the great. _Suppose one begins with tears but finishes up with joy. _Suppose one faces other's despise at the outset but receives glory at the end. _Suppose one suffers from homeless at first but finds eternal home at last. _Although God afflicts His beloved with pains first, _He ultimately comforts us, _"filled our mouth with joy, and our tongue with singing." (*Psalms 126: 2*). _We shall begin our life with the Cross but end with the Resurrection. _May I too partake of this blessing.

30 June

Go not into the way of the Gentiles, and enter not into any city of the Samaritans. But go rather to the lost sheep of the house of Israel.

Matthew 10: 5–6

Jesus' Patriotism

Jesus had a lofty, unfathomable, stern patriotism. We, his followers, too should be endowed with the same. We must love our nation as well. We should fight not against our nation's external enemies, but against its internal ones. We should be courageous to stand fearlessly against the very faces of false scholars and Pharisees, calling them, "You, hypocrites and vipers." Thus we should act with the zeal and love for our nation. But, by so doing, we shall be hated by our fellow citizens, as Jesus was despised and crossed by his people. A cross shall be burdened on us on behalf of our patriotism. Nevertheless, a nation shall be sustained only by such a patriot of faith. If we truly love our nation, we should love it as Jesus did, even though our course points to the cross.

01 July

Trust not in a friend, put not confidence in a guide; keep the doors of your mouth from her that lies in your bosom. For the son dishonors the father, the daughter rises up against her mother, the daughter in law against her mother in law; a man's enemies are the men of his own house. Therefore I will look to the LORD; I will wait for the God of my salvation; my God will hear me.

Micah 7: 5–7

I Look to Jesus

They say I am a sinner. I know I am. I LOOK TO JESUS.
They say I am a hypocrite. I may be. I LOOK TO JESUS.
They say I am ugly, am badly brought up, insolent, proud, and "too independent." I am sorry that I am. It is not all my fault. I LOOK TO JESUS.
I LOOK TO JESUS. He is I and I am He.
Let humans and churches say whatever they like about me. I am no more myself.
"The life which I now live in the flesh I live by the faith of the Son of God, who loved me, and gave Himself for me" (*Galatians 2: 20*).
And because I quote the Scripture for my defense, churches say that I am a hypocrite. I look away from churches, and LOOK TO JESUS.

02   July

Good Master, what good shall I do that I may have eternal life? And He said to him, Why do you call Me good? There is none good but one, that is, God. But if you want to enter into life, keep the commandments.

Matthew 19: 16–17

What is Good

What is good? Jesus says, "Good is God." Filial piety is good; charity is good; but these are fruits of goodness. The goodness itself is God. To know God is to become a person of goodness. To learn goodness is to approach God. We cannot know God without seeking good; we cannot become good without knowing God. Ethic and religion are two sides of one thing. The Bible defines goodness as one who "walks humbly with God" (*Micha 6: 8*). To forsake God and commit idolatry means to abandon good for doing evil, for evil-doing is true idolatry. Anyone, whether a Christian or a Buddhist, who respects righteousness and seeks goodness, is a child of God and a heir to Israel.

03 July

The LORD is my strength, and my fortress, and my deliverer; my God, my rock; I will trust in Him; He is my shield, and the horn of my salvation, my high tower.

Psalms 18: 2

Bible My Shield

The Bible has unlimited power, by which I can deserve my dignity and independence from others' attack and condemnation. The Bible is the shield of a solitary person, the fortress of a weak, the home for the person who is misunderstood. With the Bible I can stand against the Pope, Archbishops, doctors of theology, pastors and missionaries. Others may forsake and attack the Bible in order to oppose religious professionals. I will not forsake the Bible. I take refugee in the iron wall of the Bible because I know I am weak. With the Bible I can fight those who rebuke me as atheist and call me wolf. How can I forsake the strong hold of the Bible? How can I stand in the wilderness without the guard of the Bible and protect from others' arrows of merciless, shallowness, narrow-mindedness, and stiff-necked attacks?

04 July

You shall remember all the way which the LORD your God led you these forty years in the wilderness in order to humble you, to prove you, to know what is in your heart, whether you would keep His commandments or not. And He humbled you and allowed you to hunger, and then He fed you with manna, which you did not know, neither did your fathers know it, so that He might make you know that one shall not live by bread alone. But every word that comes out of the mouth of the LORD one shall live.

Deuteronomy 8: 2–3

Faith Within and Without

Faith is both internal and external. Enduring and unshakable faith only grows on the combination between the proof of external and visible conducts and the spiritual and invisible revelations. Faith is liable to fade, like a dream, if it is confined within and mystified. Or, when faith is confined without, it shall diminish and degenerate into the worldly powers of politics and economics. Like a hero, faith must stand erect on two feet, that is, the external history and nature on the one foot and the internal confidence and conscience on the other.

05 July

The LORD is good to all; and His tender mercies are over all His works.

Psalms 145: 9

Religion of Common Sense

My Christianity is the teaching of common sense. The common sense is not human wisdom, but the sense of justice and truth which God gives all human beings. I believe in Christ not because I received special miracle or had special mystic experience. I have not seen God yet. He does not manifest me Himself in dream or vision. If there is a special experience in my life, it is a special occasion that everyone has. An occasion becomes special for everyone because a person is an unique individuality… The grace of God is precious not because it is special, but because it is common. "Father in Heaven makes the sun to rise on the evil and on the good, and sends rain on the just and on the unjust" *(Matthew 5: 45)*. The sun and rain are the greatest gifts of life. The light that shines over everyone is the most precious grace in heaven and earth. I am most joyful when God graced me the same blessing as everyone.

06 July

Who now rejoice in my sufferings for you, and fill up that which is behind of the afflictions of Christ in my flesh for his body's sake, which is the church.

Colossians 1: 24

Follower's Suffering

Christ saved the whole world by His death. This is never a false statement, but the greatest truth of the truth. Christ bore and redeemed the sins of the world by His death. We, His followers, too can bear and redeem the sins of the world in proportion to the gift that God granted us. This is a blessing to be thanked wholeheartedly. By death with faith in the Lord, we can serve the world eternally, even though nothing worthy has been accomplished during the life-time. Salvation of humanity is not completed by Christ's suffering alone, but it will be completed by His followers' suffering and death through whom Christ works.

07 July

Salt is good, but if the salt has lost its saltiness, with what will you season? Have salt in yourselves, and have peace one with another.

Mark 9: 50

Peace with Salt

"Have salt in yourselves, and have peace one with another"; this is the way of peace. This teaches each one shall walk with righteousness. One shall respect other's right as well as one's own right. When one shall fulfill the righteousness with sincerity, eternal peace shall be realized. But, if righteousness is disregarded, peace shall not come. Peace is not a compromise of righteousness, but it is the full realization of righteousness. Only the peace of God has eternal endurance. Consequently, perfect peace cannot be fulfilled in this world until every human has been seasoned with salt, that is, righteousness within one's self. The secret of peace is in this word of Christ.

08 July

Blessed is the person who endures temptation, because when he or she is tried, he or she will receive the crown of life which the Lord has promised to those who love Him.

James 1: 12

Despise and Glory

Glory comes after being despised. It comes to us only after we have been ridiculed, trampled down, contemned in the face, and scorned as evil doers or hypocrites, by the people around us. Yea, despise is the forerunner of glory. We joy the hope of the crown of glory when we are despised, as spring is preceded by winter and as the full moon is preceded by an eclipse. Be not faint-hearted in the face of human's ridicule.

09 July

Our Lord Jesus Christ gave himself for our sins, that he might deliver us from this present evil world, according to the will of God and our Father.

Galatians 1: 3–4

End of Believing

Anyone who believes in Christ for the interest of one's nation will abandon Him after all. Anyone who believes in Christ for the interest of sociality and humanity will abandon Him after all. Anyone who believes in Christ in the hope of expanding the church will after all abandon Him. Anyone who adores Christ's character and believed Him will abandon Him after all. Anyone who wanted to attain to a higher thought by believing in Christ will finitely abandon Him. Anyone who sought help and consolation in troubles and hardships by believing in Christ will abandon Him after all. But the one who was shown of his sins, and cried "O wretched person that I am." (*Romans 7: 24*), and found in Christ's Cross the only way to be righteous before God, and could not but believe in Christ for its joy, such a one can not abandon Him for ever, though heavens and the earth may disappear.

10 July

Know the truth, and the truth shall make you free.

John 8: 32

Liberty Comes from God

Liberty comes from God. Anyone, therefore, who seeks to love liberty and to joy liberty, must be like God; that is, the one shall be as faithful, humble and pure as God. By thus knowing the fountain of liberty, we are disciplined not to abuse liberty. Liberty is divine because it is inherent in God.

11 July

Purge me with hyssop, and I shall be clean; wash me, and I shall be whiter than snow. Make me to hear joy and gladness; that the bones which You have broken may rejoice. Hide Your face from my sins, and blot out all my iniquities. Create in me a clean heart, O God, and renew a right spirit within me. Cast me not away from Your presence, and take not Your Holy Spirit from me. Restore to me the joy of Your salvation, and uphold me with a spirit of freedom.

Psalms 51: 7–12

Purify My Nation

Oh, God, not bless my fellow nation with riches and honors. They already possess superfluous wealth that excessively corrupted them. Oh, my God of love, not inflict further burden of sins upon them and drive them from corruption to ruin. Yea, my God, take the source of their riches and bestow upon them famine. Or, if unavoidable, open up a new volcano and let the torrents of lava cover up their houses and fields. My God of love, purify the souls of this nation by whatever measures Your will take. Only I beseech my Father, give this nation a spiritual rebirth; transform this country into the nation of true faith; revolutionize this nation like England of the 17th century.

12 July

You love Jesus Christ; in whom not yet seeing, but believing in Him you exult with unspeakable joy, and having been glorified, obtaining the end of your faith, the salvation of your souls.

1 Peter 1: 8–9

What is Faith

Faith is first of all faithfulness, second trust, and third practice. Faith without one of these essentials is not true faith. There is no other faith that brings salvation than the faith of faithfulness, trust and practice. Thus, the way of faith is clear and evident as the shining sun.

13 July

I do pray for those who shall believe on Me through their word, that they all may be one, as You, Father, are in Me, and I in You, that they also may be one in Us, so that the world may believe that You have sent Me. And I have given them the glory which You have given Me, that they may be one, even as We are one.

John 17: 20–22

What is Christianity?

Christianity is not institution, or church; neither is it creed, nor theology; neither is it the Bible, nor even the words of Christ. Christianity is a living person, Lord Jesus Christ, "the same yesterday, today, and forever" (*Hebrews 13: 8*). If Christianity is not this ever-present living Christ, it is nothing. I go directly to Him, and not through the Pope, bishops, and other priests of churches. "I in them, and they in Me," says Christ to His disciples. When this world come to the end, and the new world is created, the earthly churches shall disappear.

14 July

Behold, the days come, says the Lord Jehovah, that I will send a famine in the land; not a famine of bread nor a thirst for water, but of hearing the words of the LORD.

Amos 8: 11

God's Punishment

God's punishment, if any, shall not be failure of an enterprise, nor hard living conditions, nor sickness, nor breakdown of family, nor even death itself. None of these is to be deemed woe, unhappiness or Heavenly punishment. But God's punishment shall be the inability to know God, inability to foresee the plan of God and the Heavenly Nation, inability to understand the Bible though studied, inability to delight in thankfulness, and inability to view the providence and whole creation of God. These are, in its truest sense, the punishment of God.

15 July

Owe no one anything, except to love one another; for one who loves another has fulfilled the law.

Romans 13: 8

Debt of Life

One comes to the world indebted and grows under debts, and leaves the world by redeeming one's liabilities. Yea, one ought to leave the world after repaying one's debts. One owes one's country, one's community, one's parents, one's teachers, and one's friends. One was not born of one's own accord, has not grown by oneself, and cannot die for oneself. One as such is the product of the society and the age. One cannot reflect upon oneself and say, "I owe nobody anything." Yea, anyone who admits these liabilities and wants to redeem oneself diligently and joyfully, one is a patriot, a brave person, a dutiful child, a loyal disciple, and a true friend.

16 July

I will give them one heart, and I will put a new spirit within you. And I will remove the stony heart out of their flesh, and will give them a living heart.

Ezekiel 11: 19

Rebirth

When we hear that God's son Christ shed His blood on the cross as the sacrifice for our sins, and when we believe this, sin is no longer able to dominate over us. We therefore will break out sin, love righteousness, and seek God, our true and personal Father. Life is then full of light and joy, without any more fear of death, yet with love even towards our enemy; in fact, a great change will occur in our heart.

17 July

The rod and reproof give wisdom; but a child left to oneself brings one's mother to shame.

Proverbs 29: 15

Train Children

Blessing is a child that has stern father, mother and teacher. The true feast of truth can never be enjoyed by anyone who merely cries for liberation from "the rod and reproof" in all its forms. Modern people dislike John the Baptist, and want to approach Jesus without any rigorous training. First let us enter the primary school of righteousness, so that we may be entitled to enter the university of the Gospel. Like Andrew, first a good follower of John the Baptist could become one of the best disciples of Christ. Jesus spent His earthly life to illustrate the beginning of the Gospel. Remember this Gospel had its roots in the strictest life of John the Baptist.

18 July

For to them God would make known what are the riches of the glory of this mystery among the nations, which is Christ in you, the hope of glory, whom we preach, warning everyone and teaching everyone in all wisdom, so that we may present everyone perfect in Christ Jesus. For which I also labor, striving according to the working of Him who works in me in power.

Colossians 1: 27–29

Sole Work

What we do for Christ is nothing; what Christ does for us is everything. Our works do not justify us before God; only Christ's work makes us holy, righteous and blameless before Him. And the present-day Christianity, by emphasizing the former, makes the latter non-sense. Not charity-works, evangelical works, various and miscellaneous works connected with these works, but the life and death of Christ, especially His death upon the cross is the work for our salvation and our example. Compared with this, all other works are nothing. Yet believing in Christ's work and looking up to it, all other works bear fruit. Right and true it is that Paul said: "I determined not to know anything, save Jesus Christ and Him crucified" (*1 Corinthians 2: 2*). Christ's work was Paul's only work.

19 July

Render therefore to Caesar the things which are Caesar's; and to God the things that are God's.

                              Matthew 22: 21

Institution and Life

Institution is not compatible with life, although institution is also essential in this world. And the conflict between institution and life is inevitable. This is human life as it is. Life is a great contradiction. But beneath the contradiction there is a great harmony. Life always makes a progress under the pressure of antagonizing power of institution. The progress of life aims at the appearance of the perfection. Jesus says, "I have come so that they might have life, and that they might have it more abundantly" *(John 10: 10)*. And this life in Christ exists under outward pressure, as freedom exists with oppression side by side. Thus life abides beside institution. For institution also is what God ordained, and is therefore to be respected, rather than rejected in any way. Let it kill me first and then perfect my life. Let the world force play its influence upon me, so that my life may be perfected, just like the Lord Jesus subjected Himself to the death sentence by Pilate and Caiaphas, even to the perfection of His life.

20 July

Be perfect, be of good comfort, be of one mind, live in peace; and the God of love and peace shall be with you.

2 Corinthians 13: 11

Joy with God

How wonderful is to abide with God. There is harmony and perfection in peace, activity, righteousness, mercy, thought, and love with God; nothing is lacking. I need not to have the nature, nor human society to fill my longing. As long as I live with God of Christ Jesus, I can live as a man of absolute satisfaction.

21 July

I have heard of You by the hearing of the ear; but now my eye sees You. Therefore I abhor myself, and repent in dust and ashes.

Job 42: 5–6

True Christian

Be a true Christian, not satisfied merely with being a Church believer, or a philosophical or biblical believer. Virtually, become God's children, endowed practically with God's indwelling powers. Not merely to speak of Christianity, but to experience and practice it. I feel divine indwelling within myself, which works a fundamental change of my whole being, beyond reach of any other human or my own efforts. As a consequence, I can dread nothing in the world, and become a person, whose voice even the devil would tremble. A true Christian confesses the faith in God with Job, "I have heard of You by the hearing of the ear; but now mine eye sees You."

22 July

Consider the lilies of the field, how they grow. They do not toil, nor do they spin, but I say to you that even Solomon in his glory was not arrayed like one of these. Therefore if God so clothes the grass of the field, which today is, and tomorrow is thrown into the oven, will He not much rather clothe you, little-faiths? Therefore do not be anxious, saying, What shall we eat? Or, What shall we drink? Or, With what shall we be clothed?

Matthew 6: 28–31

Worry Not Tomorrow

Worry not your life. My God will provide for all our needs. We live in this universe of God's creation, each and everything work for our good. Why, notwithstanding then, we worry and fear of evils overtaking us? Oh, how little faith we are. Faith means true understanding of God the Creator of the universe. To spend life in endless worry, without thinking true good and beauty of life, must be an utter ignorance. Lack of faith is pity rather than evil. Even our common sense teaches us to believe in God and spend our days in peace and joy.

23   July

This is my blood of the new testament, which is shed for many. Truly I say to you, I will drink no more of the fruit of the vine, until that day that I drink it new in the Nation of God.

Mark 14: 24–25

Blood of Christ

Christ's blood, shed at His death, has already redeemed our sin and made us righteous. But it remains with each of us life-long to have His blood cleanse us from all sins. Christ's blood cleanses us, but not all at once. God's lamb has been slaughtered from the beginning of the world, and His blood will cleanse human sin to the end of the world. Redemption was done once in the past but its completion belongs to the future work. Hence, Christ's blood is needed for us, day by day, to purify our sins.

24 July

Blessed is everyone who fears the LORD, who walks in His ways. For you shall surely eat the labor of your hands; you shall be happy, and all is well with you.

                                                Psalms 128: 1–2

Value of Labor

Jesus was a laborer. I learned the value of labor through Him. Labor is important not to earn livelihood but to develop the heart. Temptation and doubt are solved only by labor, not by meditation. Labor of life is like the drainage in swamp that gets rid of rotten water and makes land fruitful. Temptation comes from much worrying and less laboring. We need not to throw ourselves in the mouth of a volcano, but just enough to serve a labor. By labor, the troubled heart like tangled thread becomes integrated and the song of praise flows out of the mouth.

25 July

I am one who bears witness of Myself, and the Father who sent Me bears witness concerning Me.

John 8: 18

See the Truth

See the truth itself, but do not expect the outcome of the truth. The outcome depends on the person who receives it. The truth does not always make a person good. Some person may become worse than before he or she encountered the truth. It is as if a candle melts under the heat of the sun, or clay hardens. The gospel of Christ may not save but destroy a nation. Nevertheless, the gospel is the truth. The truth does not depend on the outcome. It is not received by many in this world. The truth is truth even if no one recognize it. The growing number of the believer does not prove the truth of the belief. In many cases, on the contrary, the majority follows the false belief. The truth is self-evident regardless its outcome. It cannot be value-judged by the observation of social science. The truth is proved only by the son of the truth.

26 July

Faith is the assurance of things hoped for, the conviction of things not seen.

Hebrews 11: 1

Proof of Faith

Faith in its very nature is unprovable. Those Christians who try to prove faith to themselves and others are not wise because the proven faith is not faith, but sight. Faith is the belief in things not seen and therefore not proved. Many of so-called evidences of Christianity are no evidences at all. Faith is self-evidencing, and demands no proof because it "has witness borne to it." To prove faith is as difficult as to prove mathematical postulate. Nothing is so puzzling as faith to those who have it not; all the arguments in the world cannot give them proof. Therefore Jesus says, "Blessed are they that have not seen, and yet have believed" (*John 20: 29*).

27 July

You are of the Devil as your father, and the lusts of your father you will do. You are murderers from the beginning, and did not abide in the truth because there is no truth in you.

John 8: 44

Religion of Minority

The believer of Christ is one who is directed by God and seeks all matter of life for Him. This world, in contrast, is directed by the evil. The believer is of God, while this world is of devil. This is an evident reality. The world belongs to the devil utilizing science, literature, and arts. There may be some good in the world, but the total direction of the world is evil. There may be some righteous persons, but as a whole the world is of devil. Christianity is never the religion of majority. The believers are always minority. The majority is always the followers of the devil.

28 July

I hate, I despise your feast days, and I will not delight in your solemn assemblies. Though you offer Me burnt offerings and your food offerings, I will not be pleased. Nor will I regard the peace offerings of your fat animals. Take the noise of your songs away from Me; for I will not hear the melody of your stringed instruments. But let judgment roll down like waters, and righteousness like a mighty stream.

Amos 5: 21–24

Ceremony

The simpler a ceremony is, the better it is. A ceremony shall be as solemn as it is simple. The Bible does not describe about Christ's funeral service. Neither do we know how the apostles were buried. Moses, a man of God, died; and "Jehovah buried him in a valley in the land of Moab, over against Bethlehem; but no man knows of his sepulcher to this day" (*Deuteronomy 34: 6*). Yea, Witnesses of the funeral as well as the wedding ceremony is sufficient by God, the nature, and a few friends. You have no need to perform grandiose ceremony to attract the eyes of the world.

29 July

We must all appear before the judgment seat of Christ, so that each one may receive the things done in one's body, according to that which one has done, whether good or bad.

2 Corinthians 5: 10

Last Judgment

God's judgment will come; surely it will. But, instead of judging by Himself, He assigned all the judgment to His Son. We are thus judged by Christ, who is deep in compassion and forgiveness. Christ Himself preferred pardon to sacrifices, and judges humans according to the one's mercy. the criterion of Christ's judgment is human's mercy, not human's so-called righteousness and even not human's confession, proclaiming perfect diligence in dogma, ritual and evangelization. Thus, the last judgment is conducted by Christ's mercy, his compassion, his heart to pardon, his nature to grant, and his act of love. Upon this depends the eternal destiny of a human. The last judgment will be a judgment of love, and determine the destiny whether an endless torment or eternal life.

30 July

The LORD is near all those who call on Him, all those who call on Him in truth.

Psalms 145: 18

Universal Truth

I search for universal truth in my home; I study it in my soul. There is no need for me to travel abroad extensively to find it. Nor need I to attend a convention of wise people or a gathering of scholars. I seek the truth that exists before everybody. I want the light that shines upon all people. I long for the truth that fills any human beings regardless of race, nation, religion and sect. The universal truth is as deep as the human soul which can reach the depth of real existence. The worth of life, indeed, lies here in human soul, in which alone the pivotal truth of the cosmos can be revealed. Anyone, then, can discover it within one's own way and transform one's own being into a cosmic being beyond the self and the world.

31 July

Then Jesus said to His disciples, If anyone wishes to come after Me, let him or her deny one's self and take up one's cross and follow Me.

Matthew 16: 24

Faith Leaves One's Self

Faith is believing, and believing is leaving one's self in the hand of Other. It is essentially a passive state of mind, in contrast to an active state of doing. But faith, placed in the right object, begins to be active at once. It brings about good works as natural as good trees produce good fruits. Ever passive, and therefore always resting, but ever productive of good works, faith is an ideal state of existence. And it is a state which the Gospel of Christ introduces to all persons, who receive Him and believe on His name. So many false doctrines of faith are claiming to attain salvation by one's good work; but the true way to faith is to cease trying self-work, and to leave one's self as it is in His hand.

01   August

Veracity, true simplicity of heart, how valuable are these always. One who speaks what is really in one's self will find people to listen.

Carlyle, "Past and Present"

Simplicity of Heart

When I encountered the above Carlyle's words, I cried myself, "This is it, This is it." The words solved the question of my missionary. It was my mistake that I tried to lead others. It was just enough for me to witness my faith with "Veracity, true simplicity of heart." If I speak what is really in me, people will listen to me. I failed my missionary because I desired to influence others while hiding myself. Now I am determined not to influence others, but to speak just my witness about faith, sin, salvation and grace. I quit missionary and began witnessing. Behold, since then, I had no disappointment for my witnessing.

02 August

Continue in the faith grounded and settled, and are not moved away from the hope of the gospel, which you have heard and which was proclaimed in every creature under Heaven.

Colossians 1: 23

Regain of Earth

The hope of ours, who believe in Christ, is not to die and leave this world and go directly to the Heavenly Nation. It may be good, but not the best. What we do hope is to be revived after death and enabled to join Christ in the bliss of the life of righteousness upon the earth sanctified. The earth is not a place of evil from the beginning. It became cursed because the sins were committed by the human beings. Should the sins be removed, the earth would be a paradise prepared by God. What a misery is the earth which, instead of being a paradise, turned into a valley of tears. The hope of hopes is to regain the paradise upon the earth so that God's people may live therein a holy and righteous life. This is the hope of the Christian.

03 August

Therefore, brothers, we are responsible to live not after the flesh but after the spirit. For if we live after the flesh, we shall die; but if we after the Spirit do mortify the deeds of the body, we shall live.

Romans 8: 12–13

Responsibility

Responsibility makes a person serious and mature. Taking responsibility an individual becomes sincere before God and people. Responsibility is by no means painful. The true happiness of life lies in carrying out one's responsibility. Without taking responsibility a person cannot know one's calling. One cannot realize how much one can do until one is burdened by responsibility, especially of missionary. One perceives for the first time the reality of everlasting life after taking the responsibility of the missionary of God. One comes to understand the true value of the Gospel after taking the responsibility. In fact, responsibility is the heaviest burden of life. One who avoids taking responsibility is the most foolish one. Who is great? It is the person who takes heavy responsibility voluntary. Take responsibility to serve for God and people, and receive the true happiness of one's life.

04   August

Christ being come an high priest of good things to come, by a greater and more perfect tabernacle, not made with hands, that is to say, not of this building; Neither by the blood of goats and calves, but by his own blood he entered in once into the holy place, having destined eternal salvation for us.

Hebrews 9: 11–12

No Need of Ritual

Jesus Christ alone made Himself the most perfect offering to God. He alone proved Himself to be "the Lamb of God, which takes away the sin of the world" (*John 1: 29*). He also offered Himself perfectly to His Father. And now human can, by faith, take His sacrifice as one's own, so that one may offer a perfect sacrifice to God. Indeed, Jesus Christ is our perfect burnt-offering, food-offering, peace-offering, sin-offering, and trespass-offering. With His perfect offering of Himself, upon the Calvary, to His Holy Father, all the requirements for the rituals by means of oxen, sheep, doves, flour, olive oil and incense have been eternally and completely abolished. Now for anyone who believes in Him there remains none at all of the rituals to observe.

05   August

The Jews require a sign, and the Greeks seek after wisdom; but we preach Christ crucified, to the Jews a stumbling block, and to the Greeks foolishness. But to those who are called, both Jews and Greeks, Christ is the power of God and the wisdom of God.

1 Corinthians 1: 22–24

Believe First, Understand Next

Believe first and understand next. Believe in order to understand; but do not seek understanding first in order to believe because that is not the way of faith. Having no alternative but to believe is a faith. Jesus said to Thomas His disciple, "Because you have seen Me you have believed. Blessed are they who have not seen and have believed" (*John 20: 29*). Blessed are they who can believe without understanding. No human intellect can comprehend anything about God and His Holy Spirit. One cannot come to believe in Him and His works, after all, waiting to understand them. One therefore believes first. One believes the word, without doubting, simply because it is of God. This is not superstition, but a child's doubtless trust in father's. This explains what and how to believe in. But it must be mere stubbornness to refuse to believe even his father's word because of its incomprehension.

06 August

We beseech you, brethren, that you abound in love more and more, and that you learn earnestly to be quiet and to do your own labor, and to work with your own hands, as we commanded you.

1 Thessalonians 4: 10–11

Gospel for Laborer

Paul preached the Gospel of Christ as well as the Gospel of labor. And the Gospel of Christ is the Gospel of labor. Lord Christ himself was a laborer. Without love, no one knows God; and, without labor, no one can know Christ. Intellectual knowledge of God is the least worthily. Paul could learn knowledge of God better by making tents with Aquila and Priscilla than under the guidance of Gamaliel. Christianity is not a religion of priests, but of laypersons. It can be understood only with laboring by hands.

07 August

So then there remains a rest to the people of God. For one who has entered into one's rest, the one also has ceased from one's own works, as God did from His. Therefore let us labor to enter into that rest, lest anyone fall after the same example of unbelief.

Hebrews 4: 9–11

Day of Rest

The day of rest is the day that we leave our work, meditate whether we accord to God's direction, and communicate with Him. Where are we directing to and what place are we going? Rest your hands of operation, and see the stars of heave to know your place and direction. Resume your direction according to the great plan of the Creator of haven and earth. If you keep going the voyage without taking the day of rest, your ship will arrive at the unintended harbor and your life will end at total failure. The day of rest is the day of grace that God rescues us from the pitfall. Even God takes the day of rest after His creation of the universe to see its goodness. How much we should take the day of rest.

08   August

Whoever wants to be great among you, let the one be your servant. And whoever wants to be chief among you, let the one be your servant; even as the Son of man did not come to be served, but to serve.

Matthew 20: 26–28

Seek Not Big Thing

Not necessarily great writings, but small writings will do as well. Address simple and clear words of what you have seen in truth. Not necessarily great things, but little things will do as well. God sent you to this world. The earth, a creation of God, has to be made so much better before you return to your Father. Not necessarily the perfect, but the imperfect will do as well. Satisfy whatever possible consolation and joy to this suffering world, by doing your duty day by day. "Do you seek great things for yourself? Do not seek them" (*Jeremiah 45: 5*). Jeremiah thus taught his disciple Baruch. Enterprise of only great things will bring out nothing. Desire of only the perfect will yield nothing. Bearing nothing is evil doing. Great is the doing small things earnestly. Forbearance of the imperfect makes one side of the perfect. Let us do whatever we can do, with every ability and strength available, whether great or small, perfect or imperfect.

09   August

We are a savior of Christ both to them who are saved and to them who perish. To the perish we are the savior of death to death; and to the saved the savior of life to life. Who can bear these mission? For we are not as many, who corrupt the word of God; but as of sincerity, but as of God, in the sight of God speak we in Christ.

2 Corinthians 2: 15–17

Self-Contradictions

"I contradict myself [because] I am large, I contain multitudes," said Walt Whitman (*Song of Myself 51*). And God the Largest is the most self-contradictory of all beings. He is love and, at the same time, consuming fire. And His true children are always like Him. Look at Paul, Luther, and Cromwell; what combinations of self-contradictions of mother's love and father's anger they have. They never were perfect, but apparently imperfect. They were not like pink flowers on girls' breast, but were like rugged mountains fitted for giant's dwellings. And because they were imperfect and rugged, they were humankind's true friends. They demolished inequalities, banished unrighteousnesses, and laid the foundations of the Lord's Nation on earth. Alas for modern Christians, and "humanly-love" Christianity. Because they are "perfect, round, smooth, harmonious, and altogether too lovable," they are unfitted to drive deep into human souls, and to conquer nations for the Lord's possessions.

10 August

Therefore be patient, brothers, until the coming of the Lord. Behold, the farmers wait for the precious fruit of the earth and has long patience for it, until they receive the early and the latter rain. You also be patient, establish your hearts, for the coming of your Lord draws near.

James 5: 7–8

Waiting

It is good to wait. All good comes by waiting. Spring comes by waiting. Liberty comes by waiting. Peace comes by waiting. The Heavenly Nation, too, comes by waiting. When the time comes, all evil shall go and all good, instead, shall come. Therefore, you need not exert yourself to perform good, but will attain good by waiting quietly. Yet, waiting should not mean suspension but, as Milton said, "they also serve who only stand and wait" (*On his Blindness*).

11 August

No longer do I call you servants, for the servant does not know what his master does. But I have called you friends, for all things that I have heard from My Father I have made known to you.

John 15: 15

Jesus, My Friend

Nothing, indeed, can be more important in a life than to know and befriend Jesus. Though apparently hard to do, this in reality is an easy thing. To believe in a Christian dogma and to join a Christian church may sound something difficult; but nothing is difficult for anyone to have friendship with Jesus. The stronger the friendship, the deeper will be the understanding about Him, and the clearer the conception about life, even without the aid of specific study of religion or theology. As Jesus told Nathanael, "Hereafter you shall see heaven open, and the angels of God ascending and descending upon the Son of man" *(John 1: 51)*, so shall we see frequent spiritual communion between Jesus and His Father, which brings about the union of heaven and earth, incarnation of God among human beings, and spanning of an immortal bridge between this world and the world to come, whereby human can reach thither freely and safely.

12   August

We are fools for Christ's sake, but you are wise in Christ. We are weak, but you are strong. You are honorable, but we are despised. Even until this present hour we both hunger and thirst and are naked and are buffeted and have no certain dwelling place. And we labor, working with our own hands. Being reviled, we bless; being persecuted, we suffer it; being defamed, we entreat. We are made as the filth of the world, the offscouring of all things until now.

1 Corinthians 4: 10–13

Religion Changes World

Religion is neither night-dream nor day-dream. It is not vain meditation upon the infinite. Nor does it mean getting into an ecstatic state of mind for seeing god and having communion with the spirit. Religion is neither magic nor witchcraft. It is not healing of sickness by spiritual powers. It is not even what is called a miracle. On the contrary, religion is a fact that any individual can understand with common sense and can realize and practice. True religion creates great individuals. The greatest philosopher, the greatest poet, the greatest statesman, the greatest businessman, all were devout followers of a religion… Religion is concerned with the transformation of this world, however, it is not an interest of this world. Religion transforms the world deeply and fundamentally. There is, indeed, nothing so decisive as religion.

13 August

Being rooted and grounded in love, you may be able to comprehend with all saints what is the breadth and length and depth and height, and to know the love of Christ which passes knowledge, that you might be filled with all the fullness of God.

Ephesians 3: 17–19

Imperfect of World

People say this world is imperfect from top to bottom. Yea, imperfect indeed for gratifying one's lusts of the flesh. But for knowing God and for acting love, I cannot conceive of a better world than this. For keeping our patience, enlarging our generosity, and practicing love at its ultimate, there cannot be a more perfect world than this. I do not view this world as a play ground, but as a drilling gymnasium. I am not therefore puzzled at its imperfections but wish to take its advantage for perfection of my spiritual life.

14   August

You have heard that it was said, "You shall love your neighbor and hate your enemy." But I say to you, Love your enemies, bless those who curse you, do good to those who hate you, and pray for those who despitefully use you and persecute you, so that you may become sons of your Father in Heaven.

Matthew 5: 43–44

Love Enemy

Enemies are plenty against us. But we do not hate them because they are enemies, as Christ commanded to love enemy and showed the example. Friends, on the other hand, sometimes are the object of our angry. We get angry at a friend's act. We do not hesitate in blaming our friends. We get hot in arguing with friends against their repulse. But, for enemies, we take a contrary attitude. Never do we get angry at harms inflicted on us by enemies. We merely express thanks for their mockery. We try to keep silence, following our Lord, Jesus Christ, when confronted by enemy's assaults. When beaten by enemies, we pray for God's blessing upon the hand that is raised to strike us. We cherish forbearance, patience and magnanimity for our enemies. Friends, may we hate; but never enemies, whom love alone merits.

15 August

The Lord shall judge among the nations, and shall rebuke many people; and they shall beat their swords into plow-shares, and their spears into pruning-hooks; nation shall not lift up sword against nation, neither shall they learn war any more.

Isaiah 2: 4

Renunciation of War

The gospel of Jesus Christ alone can cease war. Praise the name Jehovah. Establish the height of His House firmly on all hill-tops. Give glory and supreme authority to God of Love, Father of Jesus Christ. Outside of this, we have absolutely no means of true cessation of wars. The gospel of the Cross of Jesus Christ, the gospel of the Love of God, offered for reconciliation with the betraying humanity of His own creation. Though a foolishness to the Greeks, though a stumbling-block to the Jews, though a derision to the philosopher, though a doubt to the clergy, this simple gospel alone can fulfill the only power under which all nations renounce armaments while "many people beat their swords into plow-shares and their spears into pruning-hooks, neither shall they learn war any more."

16 August

Christ who did no sin, nor was guile found in His mouth, who when He was reviled did not revile in return. When He suffered, He did not threaten, but gave Himself up to Him who judges righteously. He Himself bore our sins in His own body on the tree, that dying to sins, we might live to righteousness; by whose stripes you were healed.

1 Peter 2: 22–24

Death of Jesus

It is natural and reasonable that a person born of sin has to die, since the wages of sin is death. On the contrary, it is unnatural and unreasonable that the one like Jesus who did no sin, should have died and vanished. The death of a human does not question us, because we know he or she was born of sin. However we are dismayed if a perfect person like Jesus, who could never commit a sin and, should have died and decayed eternally. Only once, never twice, could such a person appear in human history throughout the creation. And now it becomes us to say that such a perfect person resurrected from death and ascended to heaven.

17 August

Truly, truly I say to you, When you were young, you girded yourself, and walked wherever you want; but when you shall be old, you shall stretch forth your hands, and another shall gird you, and carry you where you do not want.

John 21: 18

Successful Life

I do not do things by myself, but let things be done. I am not the director of myself, but the one who is moved by Other. I am moved, however, not by outer circumstances, but by inner commanding voice of the Spirit, which by itself carries the power to accomplish the command. I am just an instrument without particular will of my own. Let Other take hold of me, and carry me where I would not. And it is no shame to be thus controlled by the power of Other. Rather, it is the greatest of all glories for the creature to be controlled by the Creator. I know the success of my life depends upon how little I rely upon myself, and how much upon my rightful Owner.

18 August

Whosoever does not righteousness is not of God, neither one who loves not one's brethren.

1 John 3: 10

Love and Righteousness

Love is more than mercy; it has righteousness. Indeed, love is more like righteousness than anything else. We may be mistaken if we say love is righteousness; but it is nearer the truth than to say that love is mercy... . Love with righteousness is like a house with its foundation. As there is no house without foundation, there is no true love without deep and strong foundation of righteousness. God is love because He is righteous. Were He love apart from righteousness, He would be no god at all. Such a god cannot love, and His love is all false and unreliable.

19　August

Elijah said, I have been very zealous for Jehovah, God of Hosts, because the sons of Israel have forsaken Your covenant, have thrown down Your altars, and have slain Your prophets with the sword. And I alone, am left. And they seek to take my life away. _And the LORD said to him, Go, return on your way to the wilderness of Damascus.... I have left seven thousand in Israel, all the knees which have not bowed to Baal, and every mouth which has not kissed him.

1 Kings 19: 14, 15, 18

I am Not Alone

Upon the earth I am not alone to love God. I love God along with multitudes of holy people all over the world. Why should I be grieved to find no sympathizers around? I have sympathizers scattered plenteously all over the world. All the true Christians make one body in the Lord. Prayers for me are rising to the Heavenly Throne from all four corners of the world. We are workers, doing the mission under the Lord's guidance. Under whatever circumstances, therefore, we will never fall into a sentiment of loneliness or isolation.

20 August

I am crucified with Christ; nevertheless I live; yet not I, but Christ lives in me; and the life which I now live in the flesh.

Galatians 2: 20

Unity with Christ

"Christ lives within me." He stands not by my side, or lives not along with me, or stays not as my heart's guest; but He is the center of my being. This means He becomes my will and my person so as to making it impossible to distinguish Him from me, or me from Him. The relationship between Him and me, at this moment, far excels the close relationship between husband and wife. When two hearts are combined and abide together, the relationship is called friendship. But the unity between Christ and a Christian goes beyond the friendship of two hearts. It is the oneness of two persons so that the two cannot be separated eternally.

21   August

For this is My blood of the new covenant, which is shed for many for the remission of sins.

Matthew 26: 28

Right Path

The only right path to the Christian belief is the consciousness of sin. When a person is awakened to one's own sinfulness and became conscious of one's being a sinner, he or she worries one's eternal punishment, struggles how to get rid of the eternal curse, and desperately strives to find a way to salvation. And he or she will come to know the gospel of the redemption of sins as revealed by God in His Son's shedding blood upon the cross. When he or she believes this, clings to it, prays for the mercy of the Heavenly Father, and casts one's self before His presence, then he or she will realize what a Christian truth can be. For anyone who walks along this way, Christianity can never be a mere physical consolation, nor a mere philosophy, nor a mere social undertaking. The redemption of sins must be the greatest problem, determining the eternal destiny of his or her own. And when this problem is perfectly solved by the suffering of Christ's death on the cross, he or she will no longer be interested in anything else. He or she will, then, driven one's sins through Christ, came to know God.

22   August

For in Christ Jesus neither circumcision has any strength, nor uncircumcision, but a new creation.

Galatians 6: 15

Joy of Creation

God rejoices in creation; so do Christians in creating things, thoughts or new souls. Nothing else pleases them. Neither a theatre nor a leisure-travel is wanted. None of the worldly pleasures excels the joy of creation. Only the one who knows the joy of labor and creation can say: "Life is a pleasure." Make, create, and labor with hand, with word, or with knowledge at the kitchen, the factory, or the desk. "Be therefore followers of God, as dear children" (*Ephesians 5: 1*). The children of God enjoy in laboring and not ask whether big or small, or whether noble or common. They simply find joy and honor in laboring. Let's labor and create.

23   August

O the depth of the riches both of the wisdom and knowledge of God. How unsearchable are His judgments, and His ways past finding out. For who has known the mind of the Lord, or who became His counselor? Or who first gave to Him, and it will be repaid to him? For of Him and through Him and to Him are all things.

Romans 11: 33–36

Religion is Principle

Religion is not a rite, not a doctrine, not a theology, and not an institution, but a principle. Christianity, as a religion, is distinguished from other religions by its principle of life. Christianity is love, and is understood by loving. Love works into faith, and inspires on thought. Love is giving of one's self for others; God for humans, and humans for God and one another. Nothing is so simple as Christianity, and nothing so profound. A child can understand it, yet a philosopher swims in it without touching the bottom. I can be a Christian by loving, without belonging to any institutional church. "There is wideness in God's mercy like the wideness of the sea;" yes, depth too, because it is a principle and not a form and not a system.

24 August

The light shines in darkness; and the darkness comprehended it not.... That was the true Light, which lights everyone that comes into the world. He was in the world, and the world was made by him, and the world knew him not. He came to his own, and his own received him not.

John 1: 5, 9–11

Light of Gospel

One must be taught by God Himself. Teaching of humans, even of the highest and best philosophers is nothing. Wisdom of humans in its greatest brilliance is like pale reflected moon-light, and may be good for soothing life's ills, but not for healing them. By contrast, teaching of God is sunlight, full of energies, life-giving, shining by its own light, source of all power and wisdom. And we find the teaching of God in the Bible. It is sharper than the arrow of steel. One paragraph of the Book of Isaiah or a Letter of Paul is more convincing than chapters of Kant, or volumes of Schopenhauer… However, human loves darkness more than light. This is why the teaching of humans is more popular than the Gospel even in so-called Christendom. Direct light is always unwelcome to the sin-stricken world, as it is to moles and bats. The very unpopularity of prophets and apostles is a proof that they are bearers of the heavenly light.

25 August

Your Father in Heaven makes His sun to rise on the evil and on the good, and sends rain on the just and on the unjust... Therefore be perfect, even as your Father in Heaven is perfect.

Matthew 5: 45, 48

Mystery of Evil

The mystery of all mysteries is the mystery of evil. That evil does good is a sure fact of experience; yet evil is not good, and good is not evil. The very Satan is needed to make the very God a god; yet Satan is Satan, and God is God. How could that be is philosophically inexplicable, but morally and spiritually true. The worst man I have ever met in my life was one who did most to uplift me to God; and the hottest tears I ever shed were dew which gathered heavenly light into my soul. Oh mystery of life, the mystery of evil. I simply believe it, and praise God for it, all the while, without ceasing to hate evil and love good.

26   August

Beloved, if God so loved us, we ought also to love one another. No one has seen God at any time. If we love one another, God dwells in us, and His love is perfected in us.

1 John 4: 11–12

Nation of Heaven

Heavenly Nation or Paradise is nowhere else but where humans love each other. Where humans do not love each other, there can be no Paradise, even though filled with music, sermons, fervent faith or charities. To make a Paradise is least difficult. As soon as a person gives oneself up and loves humans, the Heavenly Nation is come. No need to organize a church and to establish a theology; but Paradise will come merely when a person follows Christ to love humans. Foolish are those who are busy discussing, planning and running about, but not loving people. Heavenly Nation has come. Yea, let us love people. And let Paradise appear over this sinful world, right at this moment.

27 August

I was no seer, nor was I a seer's son. But I was a herdsman and a gatherer from sycamore trees. And the LORD took me from behind the flock, and the LORD said to me, Go, prophesy to My people Israel.

Amos 7: 14–15

Great Persons

In most cases, great persons of religion have not come out of theological schools. The man of God, Elijah the Tishbite was a plain inhabitant of Giliad (*1 Kings 17: 1*). When he wanted to entrust his mission and spirit, Elijah selected Elisha, a farmer of Shaphat, who was plowing with twelve yoke of oxen before him (*1 Kings 19: 19*). Daniel was a government official. Amos was a shepherd. When God sent His Son to save the world, He did not have him learn at the school of Hillel or Gamaliel (*Acts 22: 3*), but put him in a desolate village of Nazareth, with the white peak of Lebanon and the clear stream of Kishon to teach him. Theological schools may cultivate evangelists but cannot create them. So-called evangelists out of theological schools may be unnecessary, if not harmful, for the world. Creation of great person of religion can only be done by the Creator Himself.

28 August

Jesus took the child's hand and said to her, Talitha koumi; (which interpreted is, Little girl, I say to you, arise.) And instantly the little girl arose and walked (for she was twelve years old). And they were astonished greatly.

Mark 5: 41

Jairus' Daughter

Jesus resurrected Jairus' daughter out of death and gave her back to her parents. Likewise, at the last day, Jesus will resurrect all the lost daughters and return them to the hands of the parents who believe in Him, to their inexpressible joy. All true Christians will surely experience this inexplicable joy of Jairus, at the blissful last day. All believers will certainly hear blessing words like Jairus in their own ears and will see the same powerful holy wonder by their own eyes, once in a while.

29   August

Rejoice with me, for I have found my sheep which was lost. I say to you that likewise joy shall be in Heaven over one sinner who repents, more than over ninety-nine just persons who need no repentance.

Luke 15: 6–7

Value of A Person

Churches may decline; theology may collapse; the Bible itself may be worn out. But one thing is imperishable, that is, person's soul and its liberty. The soul of a person transcends everything, and has nothing comparable among God's creation. Hence Jesus said: "likewise joy shall be in heaven over one sinner that repents." Heaven will peal with joyful cheers, like people shout for loud joy over defeat of the enemy on earth. In heaven, the heavenly host will song a triumph, and its sound will travel from star to star, even to the utter end of the universe, over the repentance of one sinner.

30 August

We are in everything commending ourselves as God's servants, in much patience, in troubles, in emergencies, in distresses, ... By honor and dishonor, by evil report and good report; as deceivers, and yet true; As unknown, and yet well known; as dying, and, behold, we live; as chastened, and not killed; As sorrowful, yet always rejoicing; as poor, yet making many rich; as having nothing, and yet possessing all things.

2 Corinthians 6: 4, 8–10

Servant of Christ

A Christian is a servant of Christ. He or she is dead to one's self; but Christ lives within him or her instead. Thus a Christian is not a person of discipline, not a person of will, not a person of meditation, but a person of heart. Yea, he or she is a person of purified heart. Therefore, to the church, the Christian may appear too wayward; to the ethicist immoral; to the philosophers ignorant. But he or she is a true person of freedom, of self-discipline, of will, of heart, of scholarship, and of poetry, because he or she is a person in whom Christ alone lives and works.

31 August

For to me to live is Christ, and to die is gain. But if I live in the flesh, this is the fruit of my labor

Philippians 1: 21

My Religion

I do not work, but believe. I do not pray, but believe. I do not sanctify myself, but believe. I do not prepare myself for heaven, but believe. Faith is believing in God's mercy and in the sacrificial death of His Son. Faith makes me work and pray; it sanctifies me and prepares me for heaven. My religion is all faith. There is no effort in it except believing. The Lord Jesus Christ is my wisdom, and righteousness, sanctification, and redemption from God (*1 Corinthians 1: 30*). He is my all. Indeed, for me to live is Christ. He by faith lives and works in me, and I become a believing one, an instrument of righteousness in His hand. All is so simple and so good.

01 September

O Land of lands. To You we give,
Our hearts, our prayers, our service free;
For You your sons shall nobly live,
And at your need shall die for You.

Whittier, J. G. "Our Country"

Two Js

I love two Js and no third; one is Jesus, and the other is Japan. I do not know which I love more, Jesus or Japan. I am hated by my countrymen for Jesus' sake as foreign belief, and I am disliked by foreign missionaries for Japan's sake as national and narrow. No matter how I may lose all my friend, but I cannot lose Jesus and Japan… My faith is not a circle with one center; it is an ellipse with two centers, Jesus and Japan. My heart and mind revolve around the two dear names. And I know that one strengthens the other; Jesus strengthens and purifies my love for Japan; and Japan clarifies and objectifies my love for Jesus. Were it not for the two, I would become a mere dreamer, a fanatic, an amorphous universal man.

02   September

But I pray to God for you not to do evil, none. And not that we may appear approved, but that you should do the good things, though we are deemed to be reprobates.

2 Corinthians 13: 7

Do Good

The best is to do good by believing in Christ; that is, to be forced by Him to do good. The second best is to imitate Christ and do good after His example. The third best is to do good, though not knowing Christ, by listening to nature's voices. Then offence to God's will because of ignorance is still pardonable. But the worst and unpardonable is to know Christ, study the Bible, teach theology, and yet to hate brothers, plot their pitfalls and inwardly delight to see their fault. God judges those who profess to be devout in faith but commit sins.

03 September

I thank my God, making mention of you always in my prayers, hearing of your love and faith which you have toward the Lord Jesus and toward all brethren, that the fellowship of your faith may operate in a full knowledge of every good thing in you in Christ Jesus. For we have great joy and consolation over your love, because the hearts of the brethren have been refreshed by you.

Philemon 1: 4–7

Letters of Love

There was no correspondence among the Oriental nations in the past. Correspondence literally does not mean mere exchange of reports. It means response, that is, I love you and you respond with the same love. Love is the meaning of correspondence. I will not write letters to let my friends know of happenings around me. Newspapers can do this. I do not write to my friends to get new knowledge. Books will do this. What I write in my letters is to let my friends know their love delighted me. This indeed is the reason why correspondence is so valuable. Without love, there is no correspondence. Love overflowing into letters is correspondence. If there is any gospel of love, this will be the letters of correspondence.

04 September

We glory in tribulation also, knowing that tribulation works out patience, and patience works out experience, and experience works out hope. And hope does not make us disappointed, because the love of God has been poured out in our hearts through the Holy Spirit given to us.

Romans 5: 3–5

Mercy and Tribulation

Mercy comes not through fortune but through tribulation. In other words, suffering must precede before receiving God's mercy. No faith and joy come without hardships just as no fire flames without fuel. Fear and anxiety precede faith as smoke precedes fire. Only when fear and anxiety burnt with heavenly fire, they turn into heavenly peace and joy in our mind. Sound faith is reached with passing through tribulations.

05 September

The Spirit breathes where He wants, and you hear His voice, but you do not know from where He comes, and where He goes; so is everyone who is born of the Spirit.

John 3: 8

Surroundings and Spirit

Surroundings though perfect can never create a Christian; but the Holy Spirit creates Christians out of most imperfect surroundings. This faithless generation thinks it possible to create a Christian in mechanical ways, by providing what they call Christian surroundings; but the Christian they thus makes is no true Christian at all, but a manufactured imitation as lifeless as any piece of fabric that comes out of their factories. Money, organizations and educational institutions cannot create a Christian. Only God by His Holy Spirit creates true Christians outside of mission-schools. The Spirit alone can and does create Christians regardless of their surroundings. The so-called "influences" have but little to do with creating Christians.

06   September

Not as though I had already attained, either were already perfect; but I follow after, if that I may apprehend that for which also I am apprehended of Christ Jesus. Brethren, I count not myself to have apprehended; but this one thing I do, forgetting those things which are behind, and reaching forth to those things which are before, I press toward the mark for the prize of the high calling of God in Christ Jesus.

Philippians 3: 12–14

Step Forward

A Christian looks not back, but ahead. He or she seeks the best not in the past, but in the future. He or she studies history, not because of his or her quest of the ideal in old sages but because of his pursuit of the origin of eternal life. The Nation of God, which the Christian is longing, comes the last. Everything, till then, is temporal and imperfect. Even historical Jesus is not the perfected Christ. "Our citizenship is in heaven; from whence also we look for the Savior, the Lord Jesus Christ" (*Philippians 3: 20*). This is a Christian life. Naturally he or she is an idealist, and is not satisfied with the past and present. He or she is an eternal youth, ever stepping forward to the front. He or she dislikes gravestones and monuments, but likes to be inspired by the heavenly hymns.

07 September

For we have no power against the truth, but for the truth.

2 Corinthians 13: 8

Follow Truth

The truth is understood not by hearing but by following it. It is especially the case of the truth of faith. Truth is not word but reality. The surest truth comes from learning by hands. One who listens to the truth but does not follow will end one's life without understanding the truth. Carlyle says, "produce and produce." One cannot understand the truth without producing, or at least trying to produce. One who avoids to follow the truth, excusing one's weakness has no understanding of the truth. One who just reads and listens but does not follow the truth will end one's life without reaching the truth. Jesus says, "My teaching is not mine, but His that sent me. If anyone will follow His will, one shall know of the teaching, whether it be of God or of myself." *(John 7: 16–17)*. The only way to prove the truth of Christianity is to follow it.

08   September

Jesus answered and said to her, Whoever drinks of this water shall thirst again, but whoever drinks of the water that I shall give him or her shall never thirst, but the water that I shall give him or her shall be in him or her a well of water springing up into everlasting life.

John 4: 13–14

Faith, Source of All

Faith ties a person to infinite God, who is the source of ethic, knowledge and skill. The person thereby reaches the source of power. Thus the person can keep ethic without regulating oneself with rules. The person who discovers the well of love within one's heart can gives others the water of life freely. Not only ethical behavior flows out of the well, but also one's understanding develops remarkably as a consequence of freedom of spirit and heart. Faith does not stay mere faith, but produces the spirit of free study as well and thereby develops science and philosophy. By faith, industry develops and business flourishes. Strike the harden rock of the heart with the stick of faith, and flow out all goodness out of the heart.

09   September

My Father works until now, and I work.

John 5: 17

Ongoing Work

Who can criticize the incompleteness of an ongoing work while a sculptor is working on the marble materials? Only at the completion of the work, the ideal and value of an artist become revealed. The analogy tells the ongoing work of God, the creator of the universe. He works now for the completion of His universe as well as human beings. We are called a son of God, but we still now repeat falling into sin. Are we a true believer? This world despises our incompleteness and doubts our incapable belief. Yet we are given the way of perfection and thereby called a son of God. We believe we will become perfected when our savior comes again with glory.

10   September

The LORD shall comfort Zion; He will comfort all her waste places; and He will make her wilderness like Eden, and her desert like the garden of the LORD. Joy and gladness shall be found in it, thanksgiving and the voice of melody.

Isaiah 51: 3

Autumn of Thanks

Ripening and harvesting Autumn has come. It is a time for thanksgiving, a time for quiet repose of all creatures, surviving the grill and drill of the summer heat, clear water of the pond, sky-high clouds, colored leaves, and plenty of fruits. All exhibit peace and joy. When the universe fills stillness of autumn and all creatures lie in harmony, it is the time for us to offer our heartfelt thanks to Heaven, and to walk along the woods and ponder upon the eternal hope.

11 September

There is no fear in love, but perfect love casts out fear, because fear has torment. He who fears has not been perfected in love. We love Him because He first loved us.

1 John 4: 18–19

True Happiness

Happiness is being loved by God. Unhappiness is being forsaken by God. True happiness first comes when our inward eye witnesses God and calls Him "Abba Father." True happiness is beyond the changes of life whether rich in knowledge of His love, or poor in spirit for His blessings. The love of God, indeed, is all about happiness of human life.

12   September

Therefore by the deeds of the law there shall no flesh be justified in the sight of God; for by the law is the knowledge of sin.

Romans 3: 20

No One is Righteous

Human cannot become good by one's own efforts and accomplishments. This is true of all truth, paradoxical as it may appear. Human's effort to get out of sin is as fruitless as an attempt of a stream to rise above the water-source, or of the sailor to steer the boat disregarding the wind. Our salvation comes from God by the medium of Christ. Without Christ, there is no reconciliation of human with God. Christ's life on earth and His death on the cross are indispensable for the salvation of our souls. Without Christ, there is no way of redemption of our sins committed against God. This is the unchanging ground of Christian faith, whatsoever reasons there may be conceived of.

13   September

The Lord is long-suffering toward us, not willing that any of us should perish, but that all of us should come to repentance.

2 Peter 3: 9

Everlasting Love

Once I sin, I will rise and go to my Father. Twice I sin, I will rise and go to my Father. Seven times I sin, I will rise and go to my Father. Seventy times seven I sin, I will rise and go to my Father (*Matthew 18: 22*). His love is everlasting. He does not wish us to perish. He never despairs of us forever. I, too, will not despair of myself, believing in His love, and will hasten today to Him immediately.

14   September

The crowds called Barnabas Jupiter, and Paul Mercury, because he was the chief speaker. And the priest of Jupiter, being before their city, brought oxen and garlands to the gates, wishing to sacrifice with the crowds. But hearing this, the apostles Barnabas and Paul tore their clothes and ran in among the people, crying out and saying, Men, why do you do these things? We also are men of like passions with you, and preaching the gospel to you to turn you from these vanities to the living God.

Acts 14: 12–15

Human is Nothing

The tomb of Moses, the servant of God, is hidden from human search (*Deuteronomy 34: 5–6*). Elijah the prophet was taken up into heaven by a chariot of fire (*2 Kings 2: 11*). Likewise God must have suffered Peter and Paul to die in an unknown place. Both were obedient servants to Christ. What they hated the most was to be worshipped by humans. God is all in all; human is nil and void. In contrast with God's fullness, human is "vanity of vanities." Human should not pretend great, to the eyes that look up to God.

15 September

Without faith it is impossible to please God, for the one who comes to God must believe that He is, and He is a rewarder of those who diligently seek Him.

Hebrews 11: 6

Faith and Love

Faith is the only way to know God and partake of His blessing. God is wise and powerful, yes all-mighty. And above all, He is love. Therefore love is the only way to know and approach the love of God. And faith is one aspect of love. This explains why, only through faith, one is saved and can please God. When we know this reality of God, we come to realize why He demands faith first. No wonder therefore the Bible, in introducing God of Love to human beings, places faith first.

16 September

My word, which goes out of My mouth, shall not return to Me empty, but it shall accomplish what I will, and it shall certainly do what I sent it to do.

Isaiah 55: 11

God of Fact

God's word tells its fact. God's argument shows a fact. God's testimony demonstrates a fact. God does not speak in vain. He speaks in silence with facts. To argue the evil of war, He speaks with the result of war. To point out the impropriety of churches, He speaks with status quo of the churches. Stop arguments, humans, but only observe, comprehend, and walk with the fact. God's word presses you, through your ears, eyes, nose, mouth, yes, from above, from below, from all corners of the earth, ever with certain fact.

17 September

The heavens declare the glory of God; and the sky shows His handiwork. Day to day utters speech, and night to night reveals knowledge.

Psalms 19: 1–2

Great Literature

True literature is the outcome of a noble idea. Mere artistic arrangement of letters cannot make a truthful literature. Like Japan's great Mt. Fuji, a great literature should not be the handiwork of a petty gardener. Heavenly inspiration lights, moves, shakes, shapes, and forces our soul to yield a true literature of profundity and sensibility. A great literature grows in the heart of a lofty spirit within and the blue sky without. A great literature come forth only where there is a guiding principle and an appreciating society.

18 September

There are also heavenly bodies and earthly bodies. But the glory of the heavenly is truly different, and that of the earthly different; ... The resurrection is sown in corruption, it is raised in incorruption; it is sown in dishonor, it is raised in glory; it is sown in weakness, it is raised in power; it is sown a natural body, it is raised a spiritual body.

1 Corinthians 15: 40–44

Spiritual Body

"Spiritual body," as called by Paul, means the embryo and kernel of Christian's resurrected body. A Christian has already received the spiritual body, which will develop into the resurrected body. A resurrected body is not something bestowed miraculously after death. But a Christian has already received the seed of a resurrected body at the time of entering into faith. And it will be completed after the death of one's natural body. Thus, for a Christian, resurrection stands as hope of future perfection as a half-accomplished fact. He or she already holds the kernel of resurrection, waiting for its perfection in glory with the Lord. A Christian is already resurrecting at this very moment.

19   September

A threefold cord is not quickly broken.

Ecclesiastes 4: 12

History, Experience and Prophecy

The Bible is a threefold cord, composed of three threads of history (past), experience (present) and prophesy (future). The Bible must therefore be understood according to these three aspects: first, historically; second, experimentally as applied to the believer's daily spiritual life, and third, prophetically as perceiving the future. Failing one or two of these, our soul's quest might feel unsatisfied, or truth might be overlooked, or superstition might creep in. Indeed, the truth of the Bible should be discovered by the three dimensions of history, experience and prophecy.

20 September

Therefore we conclude that a person is justified by faith without the deeds of the law.

Romans 3: 28

Faith Alone

Faith alone makes a person righteous. Not rites, not flesh and blood, not titles, not knowledge, and not acts, but only the faith in Jesus of Nazareth who suffered from despise and death of the Cross is the truth of truth. It may sound superstition for someone, but this is the surest truth of human experience. I believe in this, not because the Bible teaches so, but because my whole self answers it; my experience proves this; history confirms this; nature teaches this. Yes, this is faith. There is no way for human salvation without faith.

21 September

I also say to you that you are Peter, and on this rock I will build My church, and the gates of hell shall not prevail against it.

Matthew 16: 18

If he shall neglect to hear them, tell it to the church. But if he neglects to hear the church, let him be to you as a heathen and a tax-collector.

Matthew 18: 17

Jesus and Church

It is certain that Jesus had no idea of founding what we mean by the church. He expected the "little flock" that he had gathered around him to endure as such, but only till the Father's plan "to give them the Nation of God" was fulfilled... . The word "church" never occurs in the gospels, save in two passages of Matthew, one textually doubtful, both recognized by all modern scholars as belonging to that element of Matthew which is latest and has the least claim to authenticity.

22 September

As the hart pants after the water brooks, so my soul pants after You. O God, My soul t longs for You, the living God. When shall I come and appear before God?

                                                    Psalms 42: 1–2

My Soul Longs God

The time to lament is not when I am poor, neglected by the people, stay lonely in this world, or ridiculed of my ignorance. But the time to lament is when my eyes of heart lose the sight of God; when my soul loses the presence of God in the mist of doubt. Millions of treasures, then, would not make me rejoice. Fame of my name, then, throughout the world, would not satisfy me. I would then wander myself in the darkest night, even though the sun shines bright on my head. Once the sight of God were lost, I should be nothing but a corpse. My God is my love, my devotion, and my treasure more precious than my life.

23 September

I delight in the law of God after the inward person; But I see another law in my members, opposing the law of my heart, and bringing me into captivity to the law of sin which is in my members. O wretched man that I am. Who shall deliver me from the body of this death?

Romans 7: 22–24

Prisoner of Flesh

The flesh is a kind of prison. To abide in the flesh means a confinement. Human cannot have perfect liberty while in the flesh. His freedom cannot be completed until the spirit is released from the bondage of flesh through death. "The fetters of life can only be broken by death." Thus, death is the greatest emancipator, only by which the slavery of flesh shall be redeemed into the world of liberty. True lovers of freedom, therefore, shall welcome death in the same sense as Washington and Lincoln looked for liberty.

24 September

And the son arose, and came to his father. But when he was yet a great way off, his father saw him, and had compassion, and ran, and fell on his neck, and kissed him. And the son said to him, Father, I have sinned against heaven, and in your sight, and am no more worthy to be called your son.

Luke 15: 20–21

Return to Father

Upon wasting more than ten years in silly experiments and failures after my baptism, and exhausting my inner power and intellect without purpose, I was compelled to bring myself, sinful as I am, back to my Father's house, relying alone on His mercy. Without reasoning and justifying, I had to only look up to the redemption of God's Lamb, which my God had prepared for me since the beginning of the world. Oh God, I believe because I have no other way to be saved. Pardon my inexcusable sins by the power of the cross of Jesus Christ. I have none of my good deeds to offer before You. I now have no righteousness to present before You. My offering is this worn-out body and soul, this broken heart.

25 September

I in them, and You in Me, that they may be made perfect in one; and that the world may know that You have sent Me and have loved them as You have loved Me.

John 17: 23

Person of Christ

Christianity is not a system, not a church, not creed, not dogma, not theology, not the Bible, and not even the words of Christ. But Christianity is a living person of Jesus Christ our Lord, who never changes yesterday, today and tomorrow. If He does not abide forever, Christianity would then be nothing. Christianity is not a history. When Christianity is deprived of history, churches will lose their professed authority. I go to Christ directly without any human media of the church, the Pope, the clergy; or the institution. "I in them am they in Me," says Christ to His disciples.

26 September

I, John, saw the holy city, New Jerusalem, coming down from God out of Heaven, prepared as a bride adorned for her Husband... And one of the seven angels who had the seven vials full of the seven last plagues came to me and talked with me, saying, Come here, I will show you the bride, the Lamb's wife.

Revelation 21: 2, 9

Preparation for Citizen of God

We, believers, are God's servants as well as His loving children. God awaits our growth. God will not call us a friend until we become citizens of the Heavenly Nation. As long as we are on earth, we have to prepare ourselves as sinless for standing before the Lord. We shall not be ready to leave the world until this preparation is done. Neither will God let us get out of the world. But we may be allowed to leave the world any time upon completion of the preparation, as when the bride is adorned and ready to welcome the bridegroom, the Lamb. It does not matter whether we live long or short. The question is whether we are perfected or not of the preparation. Fully prepared for the bridegroom, the bride quickens the joy in his bosom.

27 September

I say to you, My friends, do not be afraid of those who kill the body, and after that have no more that they can do.

Luke 12: 4

Friends in Christ

I do not need any teachers but one. I wish all to be my friends. I do not want to have my disciples. I like them all to be my friends. The noblest relationship is that of friend, and not that of teacher and disciple. Even Christ Himself called His disciples His friends (*Luke 12: 4; John 15: 14*). We the disciples of Christ must be friends each other. Friends are equal, help each other, and teach each other. They love each other and do not worship any other than the Lord. The Oriental conception of teacher and disciple may be precious but has to perish eventually.

28   September

As concerning the gospel, Jews are enemies for your sakes; but as touching the election, they are beloved for the fathers' sakes. For the gifts and calling of God are without repentance. For as you in times past have not believed God, yet have now obtained mercy through their unbelief. Even so have these also now not believed, that through your mercy they also may obtain mercy. For God has concluded them all in unbelief, that He might have mercy to all.

Romans 11: 28–32

Universal Salvation

If ever God elected me to salvation, it must not be that I alone might be saved and the rest be lost, but that through me as a chief of sinners, many, if not all, be saved. I can be sure of my salvation only upon the condition that God is willing and able to save all sinners, that there never was, and is, and will be a sinner that God is not willing and able to save. Universal salvation as a dogma may be an offense to some particular theologians and priests, but as an individual conviction and assurance for one's final salvation, it is an extremely comforting doctrine. If God is going to save all, I am sure and certain that I too shall be saved.

29 September

Beloved, let us love one another, for love is of God, and everyone who loves has been born of God, and knows God. The one who does not love has not known God. For God is love.

1 John 4: 7–8

Ability to Love

"Love is of God, and everyone who loves has been born of God, and knows God." A great and wonderful saying. The one who loves is of God, whether be called a Unitarian, a Rationalist, a Heretic, or a Heathen; and the one who does not love is not of God, whether be called a Christian, an Orthodox, a Reverend, a missionary, a theologian, a minister, a father, a pastor, or a bishop. Love is the test of life, and whatever one's confessions and professions, only the one who loves sincerely and freely is of God and Truth. Ability to love is the greatest attainment of life; it is the unmistakable sign of the possession of eternal life.

30 September

With humans it is impossible, but not with God; for with God all things are possible.

Mark 10: 27

Great Demands

It is written: "Be perfect, even as your Father in heaven is perfect" (*Matthew 5: 48*). Again, "be holy, for I am holy." (*1 Peter 1: 16*). Is it possible for weak, imperfect humans to meet so great demands? It is not possible by their own efforts, but possible by the power of Almighty Father. "Be perfect" means "Submit yourselves to be perfected by Him." God is able to create us, and build us the image of His Son by sending the Holy Spirit. What is called Christian morality is to be with God and His Christ; as it is also written: "Apart from Me, you can do nothing" (*John 15: 5*); and "With God all things are possible."

01   October

All scripture is given by inspiration of God, and is beneficial for teaching, for lesson, for correction, for instruction in righteousness;

2 Timothy 3: 16

Return to Bible

Autumn has come. I will come back to the Bible. To the Bible that is of heaven and not of the world. To the Bible that pertains to the spirit and not to the flesh. To the Bible that is for the whole of humanity and not for the church alone. With a spirit of freedom I will return to it. With an attitude of a seeker after the truth I will return to it. And I will make a step forward in understanding God, liberty, and everlasting life.

02 October

Give ear, O heavens, and I will speak; and hear, O earth, the words of my mouth. My teaching shall drop as the rain; my speech shall drop down as the dew, as the small rain on the tender plant, and as the showers on the grass;

Deuteronomy 32: 1–2

Silence

Silence reigns in the nature and abides in the Bible. I am comforted, when a lonely flower drops its head, laden with the weighty dew. Turmoil of my inner affliction become silent by a verse of the Holy Scripture. I find solace in little flowers and calm in the old Bible when a great sensation angers around me.

03   October

We have known the love of God, because He laid down His life for us. And we ought to lay down our lives for the brothers.

1 John 3: 16

Miracle of Love

We are saved by faith, and not by deed. Salvation comes by faith in the unbounded love of God. It is reasonable that God saves the righteous. But it is miracle that God reconciled Himself to sinners, cleansed their sins and made them His children. This love far exceeds what we can conceive, and is what we think most incredible. Hard to believe is not physical miracles such as turning water into wine or resurrecting the dead into living, but the miracle of love which takes sins away from sinners, and gives them a pure heart instead of condemning their sins. This is the love of God; and we are saved by believing in this Love. The Gospels describe this Love. Christians believe in this Love. Our peace rests in this Love. We are safe in this Love. I firmly believe in this Love of God in pursuit for a child of God.

04   October

Let each one remain in the calling in which one was called. Were you called as a slave? It does not matter to you, but if you are able to become free, use it rather. For one who is called a slave in the Lord is a freed person of the Lord. And likewise, one who is called a free person is a slave of Christ. You are bought with a price, do not be the slaves of humans.

1 Corinthians 7: 20–24

Stay Your Vocation

Stay your vocation. Do not change it by yourself, but walk with God. This is not determinism, but the way to live in this world, where our ideal is hardly realized and the unrighteousnesses are its nature. Do not put yourself on the luck; give yours joyfully if others demand it. Stay with God. Wait the time when God reveals you. Accept the vocation if God calls you to it in this world. God unfailingly calls us to a precious vocation in His holy Nation, therefore we do not seek the fame of this world. We stay a given position in this world and content with knowing and walking with God. We will wait until Christ comes again and gives us a predestined position in other world.

05   October

You shall have no other gods before Me... For I the LORD your God am a jealous God.

Exodus 20: 3, 5

Wholehearted Love

God is supreme love. Hence He demands of man and woman unreserved and unconditional love. This is His rightful demand, for God confronts us with such love. God gives us all creatures. Everything that we receive is God's gift. The love of God, therefore, demands of us single-minded trust and wholehearted love. Is there any demand more reasonable? Jealous God is another name of the God of Love. We console ourselves with the near presence of the God of unlimited love.

06   October

Let your word be, Yes, yes; No, no. For whatever is more than these comes from evil.

Matthew 5: 37

Yes and No

I like to be positive, and not to be negative. I like to say Yes always, and never to say No. But in this world of self-contradictions, of uncertainties and darknesses, it is not possible to say Yes always and never to say No. But Yes without No is nothing. I must love God and hate Satan. But where few have courage to say No, my No may be taken for Nihilism and Anarchism. But I must say No that my Yes may be effective, and God's name be glorified in this dark world. As in the art of Rembrandt, the light of life shines brilliantly only on the background of deep shades.

07   October

We all come into the unity of the faith and the knowledge of the Son of God, to a full-grown adult, to the measure of the stature of the fullness of Christ; so that we no longer may be infants, tossed to and fro and carried about by every wind of doctrine, in the dishonesty of humans, in cunning craftiness, to the wiles of deceit. But that you, speaking the truth in love, may in all things grow up to Him who is the Head, even Christ.

Ephesians 4: 13–15

Faith and Knowledge

The world has full of misconceptions; but no more distressing than the separation between faith and knowledge. Faith claims "faith alone"; and knowledge also does itself alone; then both cease to grow and die away. Faith without knowledge turns into superstition, whereas knowledge without faith into mere mechanism. Future civilization, as it is to say, may be termed as the sad separation between faith and knowledge. But I shall postulate that, from the insight of the Bible's following saying: "What therefore God has joined together, let not human separate" (*Matthew 19: 6*), faith is wife and knowledge is husband. Then wife and husband are no longer two, but one. Husband appreciates wife; and wife does husband. Separation between wife and husband brings about the destruction of life. The same is the case of faith and knowledge. Faith inspires knowledge, and knowledge clarifies faith. The separation of faith and knowledge collapses a civilization. In the world we have nothing more dreadful than a knowledge without faith and a faith without knowledge.

08   October

I will not drive them (the Hivite, the Canaanite, and the Hittite) out from before you in one year, lest the land become desolate, and the beasts of the field multiply against you. By little and little, I will drive them out from before you, until you be increased, and inherit the land.

Exodus 23: 29–30

Perfection and Humbleness

Perfection is the greatest possible attainment of life. But perfection has its dangers. Perfection breeds us pride and self-satisfaction. Imperfection rightly used creates us a humble heart of Christ. Because imperfect, we humble ourselves and take our refuge in the Cross of Christ. It must be for this reason that perfection is attained very slowly in our actual life as God said to the children of Israel through Moses. By little and little the Merciful Father will drive imperfections out from within our hearts, lest by becoming perfect suddenly, worse character may multiply against us than the imperfections of flesh and mind. May Lord's will be done in matter of our perfection, as in every thing else.

09   October

Your word is a lamp to my feet, and a light to my path.

Psalms 119: 105

Season of Reading

Autumn affords many a lovely night for reading under the lamp. The first to be read is the Bible. It cherishes eternal gains. By reading the Bible, human becomes youth though aged. Everlasting Spring abides in the heart. By reading the Bible, there never lacks an idea. From my mouth will then flow out a poem, a song and a tune of praise. Reading the Bible enhances quest for knowledge. Unlimited longing for understanding goes after the wider and deeper truth of the universe and humanity. If ever there exists God's word, I think it is the Bible. Books are the best treasures of the human race; and the highest treasure of treasures must be the Bible.

10   October

It happened to me, traveling and drawing near to Damascus; suddenly, about midday, a great light out of the heaven shone around me. And I fell to the ground and heard a voice saying to me, Saul, Saul, why do you persecute Me? And I answered, Who are you, lord? And he said to me, I am Jesus of Nazareth, whom you persecute.

Acts 22: 6–8

Witness of Conversion

Preaching of Christianity is simple. It is not to say, "Repent," but "God has blessed me as I am. I want to witness this joy to you." Evangelism, if it is of God, must be always like this. Paul preached the gospel like this, as he repeated confession of his conversion before his audience, which the Bible minutely describes. This also explains why his letters are self-explanatory and not instructive. Rich knowledge of theology does not make an evangelist of Christianity. An evangelist should not speak to the world unless one owns spiritual experience which must be submitted to the world.

11 October

A great and strong wind tore the mountains, and broke the rocks in pieces before the LORD. But the LORD was not in the wind. And after the wind was an earthquake, but the LORD was not in the earthquake. And after the earthquake was a fire, but the LORD was not in the fire. And after the fire was a still, small voice.

1 Kings 19: 11–12

Small Still Voice

Know that, though God employs great wind, He is not like great wind. Rip and smash is not what He delights. Nor is He like an earthquake. Shake and terrify is not what He aims. Nor is He like fire. Burning to ashes is not what He wants. God loves stillness. His throne is midst the stillness of the universe. His voice is not like the waves but like the creeks. He roars not, but whispers. When we sit in silence and hear a still voice, we know it is truly God's voice.

12   October

You will be hated of all humans for My name's sake, but the one who endures to the end shall be saved.

                                         Matthew 10: 22

Alone with God

People hate each other and are hated each other. God alone loves a person. Every person is alone. One's loneliness is not dissolved until God is with the one. "I am not alone, because the Father is with Me," says Jesus (*John 16: 32*). This is the same words of all those who experienced the depth of life. One does not hate anyone any more, but can love anyone because one lives alone with the great Partner. Be alone first of all, and you will be alone with God and love every person. Be alone truly without a church, and you will find the invisible church of God's Universe. Alone, not only I but everyone is alone. And aloneness is the way of grace to reach God. A person cannot reach to God in group, but the way to reach God is individual. A person dies as an individual and enters the Nation of God as an individual. One leaves others, goes to God, and enters into the intimate relationship of love with Him.

13 October

Therefore I say to you, Take no thought for your life, what you shall eat, or what you shall drink; nor yet for your body, what you shall put on. Is not the life more than meat, and the body than clothes? Behold the fowls of the air; for they sow not, neither do they reap, nor gather into barns; yet your heavenly Father feeds them. Are you not much better than they?

Matthew 6: 25–26

All Comes from God

God clothes and feeds me. I need not snatch my daily necessaries out of others' hands. My bred and clothes are granted to me as rain falls on the trees and the grass. Sufficient is for me simply to work and wait quietly for God's blessing. My thoughts come from God. No need for me to search for the truth in heaps of dust-covered books. God's truth visits my heart like the gentle wind that touches green leaves. Sufficient is for me simply to pray Him and hear His voice. God accomplishes my work. I dare not blow my trumpet before people. My work is completed without self-endeavor, like a fruit is sun-lit and ripened without self-effort. Sufficient is for me merely to sow seeds quietly, water them and wait for their fruition.

14 October

The Jew of outward is not a true one, nor is circumcision in the flesh true one: But a true Jew is one inwardly; and true circumcision is of the heart, in the spirit, and not in the letter; whose praise is not of humans, but of God.

Romans 2: 28–29

Japanese Christianity

Japanese Christianity is not Christianity peculiar to Japan. It is the Christianity which a Japanese receives directly from God without an intermediary foreigner. It is self-evident. In the same sense, there is German Christianity, or English Christianity, or Scottish Christianity, or American Christianity. Each country has her Christianity. And there must be yea, Japanese Christianity. There is Japanese Christianity where the spirit of a Japanese has inspired with the breath of the Almighty *(Job 32: 8)*. This Christianity is free, independent, creative, and productive. No person was ever saved by other persons' faith, and no nation will ever be saved by other nations' religion. True Christianity should be like this. Japanese Christianity alone can well save Japan and the Japanese.

15   October

If a brother or sister be naked and lacking of daily food, And one of you say to them, Go in peace, be warmed and filled; notwithstanding you do not give them those things which are needful to the body; what good is it?

James 2: 15–16

Compensation and Salvation

You may further ask me, "Why not God can save human unless He Himself suffers?" I would ask you, "Why not John Howard could improve prisons in Europe by sitting quietly in his home? Why not Livingstone could save Africa people by merely offering fervent prayers in his native land?" Salvation of a sinner without redeeming the sin is fruitless as to say to a needy person "Go in peace" without giving the one food and clothes. Faith without deed is dead faith. Deliverance from a sin without redemption is a false claim. The cross of Christ is a living evidence of God's love.

16   October

Rejoice according as you are partakers of Christ's suffering, so that when His glory shall be revealed, you may be glad also with exceeding joy.

1 Peter 4: 13

Joyful Christian

A Christian rejoices always; not only when exulted but also when distressed. A Christian conquers distress with joy. He or she even rejoices over long-suffering. Not to abandon difficulties, but to transform it for nearing to God's perfection. A Christian does not count suffering a loss, but a great gain. Suffering does not crush but deepens a Christian heart. Anyone who complains distress as an evil cannot understand a Christian. A Christian heartily joy suffering, because God's greatest blessing abides in suffering and the supreme happiness of human life comes through it.

17   October

Truly I say to you, If you have faith and do not doubt, you shall not only do this miracle of the fig tree, but also; if you shall say to this mountain, Be moved and be thrown into the sea; it shall be done. And all things, whatever you shall ask in prayer, believing, you shall receive.

Matthew 21: 21–22

Power of Prayer

There are the power of money, of politics, and of wisdom; but none of these can come up to the power of prayer. This, indeed, is the power of sincerity, which can penetrate a mountain and crush a rocky crag. All the works on earth, which are called great, have been accomplished by the power of prayer. A country not established on the power of prayer is a false country, ungrounded on an eternal and unchanging basis. Any art without the power of prayer can never bear the heavenly ideal. Prayer is the only secret key to open and enter the spiritual life. So there should be never expected anything worth the name "great," whether a great statesman, a great artist, a great literature, or a great discovery etc., out of a nation without prayer.

18   October

O LORD, what is human whom You take care of? Or what is the son of human whom You make account of? Human is like vanity; one's days are like a shadow that passes away.

Psalms 144: 3–4

Contradiction

I know well I am a contradicted person, and not a well-balanced and spotless person. Yet I do not attempt to make up my contradiction. For the problem is not specifically of mine, but of the life at large in this world as the Bible teaches. Contradiction is a reality of life; this should be accepted as a fact. If you turn your eyes from the reality because of the fear of contradiction, you will come to believe nothing. Walt Whitman, an American poet, says, "I contradict myself [because] I am large, I contain multitudes " (*Song of Myself 51*). Everyone is created in the image of God and thus is an eternal being. Therefore contradiction is inevitable. Be contradicted not from evil-mind, but from good will. Be contradicted not as a child but as a matured. Be not afraid of contradiction.

19   October

Blessed are they who have been persecuted for righteousness sake. For theirs is the Nation of Heaven.

Matthew 5: 10

Suffering and Faith

One may come to Christ because he or she suffered. Another may suffer because he or she came to Christ. There are deep relationships between suffering and faith. Suffering first and faith next is lower faith, while faith first and suffering next is higher. In reality, however, 99 per cent of faith comes after suffering in order to be rescued from it. There are few faith which bring about suffering like the stars in rainy night. It is evident what God pleases is the faith that brings about suffering, not the faith for consolation of suffering.

20 October

This is life eternal, that they might know You the only true God, and Jesus Christ, whom You have sent.

John 17: 3

Purpose of Life

The purpose of life is to know God. And if suffering is essential for attaining to this aim, it is not a misfortune but a blessing. Job's suffering accomplished this honorable attainment. Likewise, we too, passing through tribulation, shall arrive at this worthy aim. Jesus Himself was made "perfect through sufferings" (*Hebrew 2: 10*). May we become like Jesus through suffering.

21 October

If you keep My commandments, you shall abide in My love, even as I have kept My Father's commandments and abide in His love.

John 15: 10

Keep Commandments

Filled with Holy Spirit, we shall first abide in God's commandments. Prayer alone or Study of the Bible alone is not enough for faith. Abide in God's commandments with firm determination and courage, and you will be bountiful flow of the Holy Spirit, God's greatest gift for His children. The gift of the Holy Spirit can only be poured by our acts of faith. Study creates holy desire; prayer calls for it; and practice realizes it. Practice indeed is the most powerful prayer.

22   October

We are the circumcision who worship God in the spirit and rejoice in Christ Jesus and have no confidence in the flesh.

Philippians 3: 3

Heart of a Christian

What is the heart of a Christian to tide over life? It is to die of the flesh and to live of the spirit, that is to say, to die one's own ego by the work of the Holy Spirit. Then any suffering will become blessing with joy and peace in the heart. We can be the righteous, shedding light upon the darkness around. Not alone Christians, but any Christian's neighbors also can enjoy the grace. This is the true path to the blessed home and society. Let each one of us be a light and a spring of the grace, so that every home and every society can be blessed.

23   October

When the gentiles, who do not have the Law, do by nature the things of the Law, these, not having the Law, are a law to themselves; who show the work of the law written in their hearts, their conscience also bearing witness, and the thoughts between one another accusing or even excusing one another, in a day when God shall judge the secrets of humans by Jesus Christ according to my gospel.

Romans 2: 14–16

Religion of Conscience

Christianity, after all, is a religion of conscience. As long as human has a conscience, and commits sin, Christianity cannot be cast out. Through the remission of sins by Christ, human can have true peace. The way of God that justifies sinners as righteous and redeemed them is only in Christianity. This is not the question of whether one agrees with science. But this is the question of whether one can have peace with one's conscience. Howsoever explained about its source, conscience is conscience; and human cannot decline its command. With sharpened conscience, anyone can reach Christianity. I too owed to take this way and believe in Him. The highway through the universe is driving a person toward Christ. Kant's "Stars ahead and moral law within" will be enough to make a person a Christian. Moral law leads to religion of conscience and religion ends in Christianity, namely, the way of Christ's cross. I followed this way to become a Christian.

24   October

Behold, they say, Our bones are dried and our hope is lost; we are cut off by ourselves. Therefore prophesy and say to them, So says the Lord Jehovah; Behold, O My people, I will open your graves and cause you to come up out of your graves, and will bring you into the land of Israel.

Ezekiel 37: 11–12

Question of Other World

Written to a father who grieved over the death of his 7–year-old daughter, much to his concern about her future life: "There are many unsolvable problems in human life. No human throughout the world, can ever explain these questions satisfactorily. But we know one thing, that is, God is Love. And that the God of Love can never, in the world to come ill-treat the ones whom we love here. The Bible says Christ died for all the people. Not even a single person, in the universe, can be out of the grace of Christ's redemption. All that the Bible teaches us is to believe and bring to the conclusion: God is Love."

25 October

Lord, behold, Lazarus whom You love is sick. When Jesus heard, He said, This sickness is not to death, but for the glory of God, so that the Son of God might be glorified by it.

John 11: 3–4

Grace of Sickness

Sickness of the body is the rest of the spirit. We could not help but taking rest during sickness. Therefore sickness is a great grace, while the time of health is of working. For the servant of God, the healthy body is to serve for God and people, not for one's own. We have to serve others from arousing up to going to the bed, without considering one's self. But we are excused from this duty as soon as we are struck by sick and lie down the bed. The time of sickness is ours, and we can think of own self and communicate with God intimately. It is our rest when our legs do not move, our hands do not work, and our throat does not make voice. Our rest is during sickness, not after sickness. Once recovered from sickness, we immediately begin to work. Thus the sickness of the servant of Christ is for rest.

26 October

You have need of patience, so that after you have done the will of God you might receive the promise.

Hebrews 10: 36

Patience

Patience means to walk strait forward, whether the time is in season or not, whether praised or ill spoken, whether approved or opposed, whether succeeded or failed. Walk straight forward to the command of God without hesitating or turning to the right or to the left. Patience needs time and long-suffering to keep working one thing. It cannot avoid simpleness and plainness. It is like breaking through a great rock by drilling with all effort and continuity. Patience needs steadfastness. We cannot have patience as long as we attempt to make compromise with or to please this world. The road of patience is not the path of pleasure in the world.

27 October

Now I beseech you, brethren, mark them which cause divisions and offences contrary to the teaching which you have learned; and avoid them. For they that are such serve not our Lord Jesus Christ, but their own belly; and by good words and fair speeches deceive the hearts of the simple. For your obedience is come abroad to all person. I am glad therefore on your behalf; but yet I would have you wise to that which is good, and simple concerning evil.

Romans 16: 17–19

Protestantism

I am a Protestant. I protest against Roman Catholicism. I protest against English Episcopalianism, against German Lutheranism, against Scottish Presbyterianism, against American Congregationalism, Methodism, and Baptism, against every one of over six-hundred sects and isms that go under the name of Protestantism. Yea, I protest against my own ism, if I have any. The gospel I believe in is Jesus Christ and Him crucified; and I protest against any doctrine which goes beyond, or does not come up to, this simplest of all doctrines. Protestantism, I understand, is Christ versus human desires, faith versus churches. Simplicity of faith warns against complexities, living life opposes dead organizations.

28　October

All that the Father gives Me shall come to Me, and the one who comes to Me I will in no way cast out. For I came down from Heaven, not to do My own will but the will of Him who sent Me. And this is the will of the Father who sent Me, that of all which He has given Me I should lose nothing but should raise it up again at the last day.

John 6: 37–39

My Faith

I do not attempt to propagate my faith to others, rather I wait someone to come to me voluntary. Even then, I do not accept all of those who come to me. I speak them the difficulty of faith in Christ, especially for those who are attracted by my personality. I let them know my enemies and their accusations. I do not want to speak my faith anyone but the person of sincerity, who is compelled to come to me. I do not have a power to make just one person a Christian even by all my means and efforts. I believe that ones whom God Himself called comes to Christ unfailingly in spite of all difficulties and obstacles, and stay with Him for ever. I believe that only the spirit of God makes a person a Christian, and not any means and effort of humans. I pray that I can take part in the holy project of God, but by no means I make effort to gain power and influence on this world.

29 October

We also have a more sure word of prophecy, to which you do well to take heed, as to a light that shines in a dark place, until the day dawns and the Daystar arises in your hearts.

2 Peter 1: 19

History and Prophecy

It is untrue that statesmen and warriors make history. They ruffles on the surface of human history; but the force of history is the mighty purpose of God as revealed through His prophets. The secular rulers such as Nebuchadnezzar, Alexander, Caesar, Napoleon, Kaiser Wilhelm II, or Woodrow Wilson, were all ripple-raisers, remembered only by the foams and bubbles left by them on the steady current of history. Humans call them "great," but God calls them mere a creature "whose breath is in their noses" (*Isaiah 2: 22*). Congresses and human intuitions can never make true laws; they simply express the wills and desires of the people, too often unholy and shamefully selfish, entirely contrary to the holy law of God. Surely then we need pay no attention to what they did and do, but take heed to "a more sure word of prophecy."

30   October

Give, and it shall be given to you, they shall give into your bosom, good measure pressed down and shaken together and running over. For with the same measure that you measure, it shall be measured to you again.

Luke 6: 38

Give First

Comfort first, and you will be comforted. Help first, and you will be helped. Give first, and you will be given. Just as the Lord said: "Give, and it shall be given to you… With the same measure that you measure, it shall be measured to you again." You will be never comforted, when you lament your weakness, insufficiency, and pain. Do you want to be comforted? Go and comfort the suffered persons. Do you want to be helped? Help the weak persons. Do you want to be given? Give to the poor. Give first, and you will receive. You shall be measured with the same measure that you measure.

31 October

But of God are You in Christ Jesus, who of God is made to us wisdom, and righteousness, and sanctification, and redemption.

1 Corinthians 1: 30

Faith in Christ

Christ stands for our righteousness, holiness and redemption. He is my moral law, faith and salvation. He accomplished all what I ought to do for God. I am unrighteous but, by believing in Christ, I can stand before God, as His righteous one. I am corrupted but, by believing in Christ, I can stand before God as His holy one. My salvation is not yet perfected, but I am counted as one saved by the faith of Christ. Salvation is completed by God through faith. This may be a stumbling block to the Jews or foolishness to the Greeks. But, to the called, this is the truth and the power (*1 Corinthians 1: 23*).

01 November

Now a righteousness of God has been revealed apart from Law, being witnessed by the Law and the Prophets; even the righteousness of God through the faith of Jesus Christ... For all have sinned and come short of the glory of God, being justified freely by His grace through the redemption that is in Christ Jesus.

Romans 3: 21–24

Paradox of Faith

Faith is a great paradox and a grand truth. One can be justified by faith as such, not by works or even not by the result of faith. No work can justify a person before God. But if I have faith, my justification is assured, and I am saved although I make no convert, and feed no beggar in my life. Faith gives me peace, and peace gives me strength; and though I rely not upon works, something of eternal work comes out of my life. It is a paradox of faith: denying works, works come by themselves. It is a refutation of all doctrine of salvation by works, of Roman Catholicism, and of modern American Christianity.

02 November

In the beginning was the Word, and the Word was with God, and the Word was God. He was in the beginning with God. All things came into being through Him, and without Him not even one thing came into being that has come into being. In Him was life, and the life was the light of humans.

John 1: 1–4

Spirit of Universe

Sacrifice is the Spirit of the Universe. Jesus Christ is the most perfect manifestation of this spirit. The Bible says, "God created all things by Jesus Christ" (*Ephesians 3: 9*). That is, God created the Universe according to the norm of Christ. For one who knows Christ knows God; one who understands the Cross understands the Universe. Thus we understand the Universe through following after Christ and walking the life of sacrifice.

03 November

For in Christ dwells all the fullness of the divine bodily. And you are complete in Him, who is the Head of all principality and power

Colossians 2: 9–10

Jesus Christ

The essence of Christianity is faith and Christ, as Paul says: "Christ Jesus, who is of God is made to us of wisdom, righteousness, sanctification, and redemption" (*1 Corinthians 1: 30*). To learn Christianity, therefore, we do not need to go to Oxford or Harvard University. Neither need we to ask of the Pope of Rome or the archbishop of Canterbury. The theology of the faithful is Jesus; their baptism is Jesus; their perfection is Jesus. Yea, Jesus Christ is all. Christianity is not the church, not the bishop, not the presbyter, nor theology and dogma. We can simply believe in Jesus and can at once reach the heart of Christianity.

04   November

Jesus said to them, He that is without sin among you, let him first cast a stone at her... And they which heard it, being convicted by their own conscience, went out one by one, beginning at the eldest, even to the last; and Jesus was left alone, and the woman standing in the midst. When Jesus had lifted up himself, and saw none but the woman, he said to her, Woman, where are those your accusers? Has no man condemned You? She said, No man, Lord. And Jesus said to her, Neither do I condemn You; go, and sin no more.

John 8: 7–11

Morality

Moral is relative. We have to put ourselves in his or her position when we lead a person to morality. Not by command but by example, we have to help him or her realize divine rules according to and within his or her capacity. Never should we sit high, like the Pharisees, and give forth commands. But, we should guide him or her to the ideal lowering ourselves, keeping ourselves in his or her situations, taking his or her hands, and carrying his or her feet. This in fact is the way our Savior Jesus Christ conducted. He taught the Samaritan woman, not by admonishing her immoral conduct and forcing upon her anything beyond her power. He guided her to the spring of real life according to her capability. Jesus was the greatest moralist. He erred not in teaching morality to humans. Morality is a way from the lower to the higher. To maintain this, fatherly dignity and motherly tenderness must be needed. We should not take morality as father's strict and relentless command alone.

05 November

Be not conformed to this world; but be transformed by the renewing of your heart, that you may prove what is that good, and acceptable, and perfect, will of God.

Romans 12: 2

Revolution from Within

Revolution must begin within one's self. Though tons of liquid may be absorbing crystalline matter, solidification starts only when a solid matter is thrown in the liquid. Commanding cannot force water to solidify. Scolding has no avail. Let me first be the foundation of solidification. Crystallization will then start from myself. Let me stand firm upon the cornerstone of the universe. All others will then come around me gradually to get orientated in line with me. This indeed is the great secret of successful innovation.

06 November

I looked, and there was none to help; and I wondered that there was no one to uphold; therefore My own arm has saved for Me; and My fury upheld Me.

Isaiah 63: 5

Stand Alone

We need not to belong a church at all to serve Christ. We by alone can devote ourselves for Christ. Christ is the lord of salvation for everyone. We are one of the redeemed. We by alone can hold the light in the world since we receive Christ in our heart. We can stand alone on the steep rock and become the light of ship guard in the darkness. Further standing alone we can comfort other solitary persons, who are not rare in the world. There are many persons who weep and sorrow for their unbearable solitariness. Therefore it is an important work to inform them the blessing and holiness of a solitary person. Being alone we become a guider for millions of the solitary person in the world

07 November

You must not be called Rabbi, for One is your teacher, Christ, and you are all brothers. And call no one your father on the earth, for One is your Father in Heaven. Nor be called teachers, for One is your Teacher, even Christ. But one who is greatest among you shall be your servant.

Matthew 23: 8–1

Take Off Pretension

Take off pretension of dignity. Let us be as we are. Vain honors and titles lead to mistrust, devoid of confidence. Real independence cannot be achieved by pretension. Renewal of the spirit cannot be accomplished by showing false power. Pretension of dignity has no real power. Name does not represent reality. Contention and corruption come mainly from pretension of dignity, borrowing a nominal title of authority. We are the weakest when we make a bluff in false power. Destruction of pretension will not threat us, for what has to fall should fall. A firm house can only stand on a solid rock.

08 November

Be enriched in everything to all generosity, which works out thanksgiving to God through us. For this service not only supplies the things lacking of the saints, but also multiplying through many thanksgivings to God.

2 Corinthians 9: 11–12

Bountiful with Rejoice

Be thoroughly bountiful with God's mercy, to the fullness of joy and gratitude, and have permeated with the same joy to the world. For this world is full of cries of dissatisfaction and groans of disappointment. Voices of praise of God's people offset these cries and groans. Who would rejoice, without our rejoicing? As is written, "Praise is comely for the upright" (*Psalms 33: 1*). Remember that we have responsibility to turn our native soil as well as the whole world to God-praise-ward. Rejoicing and thanksgiving make the keynote of Christianity. Thanksgiving penetrates through the Christian life. Thanks for good as well as for evil. The greatest thanks of human life are that God be with us. "You are with God. What else do you need?"

09   November

Jesus took bread, and gave thanks, and brake it, and gave to them... And he took the cup, and gave thanks, and gave to them; and they all drank of it.

Mark 14: 22–23

Thanksgiving of Daily Bread

All bread is the gift of God. We receive it with thanks because we have not earned it by ourselves. Here lies Christian's thanksgiving of a meal. Christ did not take meals without thanksgiving beforehand. Rembrandt illustrated young Christ in front of a simple table bearing a few loaves of bread, with eyes turned heavenward. This means Christ's thanksgiving before His meals. The Christian takes one's meal with thanksgiving because it is the manna from Heaven (*John 6: 31*). We are grateful when we pray, "Give us today our daily bread." (*Matthew 6: 11*). Thanksgiving is an expression of faith. Lack of thanksgiving is the lack of faith. Give thanks to God for His mercies.

10 November

The LORD, my refuge and my fortress, my God; in Him I will trust. He shall cover me with His feathers, and under His wings I shall trust. His truth shall be my shield, and buckler. I shall not fear the terror by night.

Psalms 91: 2–5

Way of Faith

Simple is the way of faith. It suffices just to entrust God. Light will then come on me, power added to me, sin taken from me, and the Holy Spirit will abide in me. Faith is the way of perfection. Faith is not wandering along the path of knowledge and climbing the hill of ethic, but flying directly to the bosom of God like an eagle with wide-spread wings. Knowledge may be the lamp to illuminate darkness; virtue may be the stick to search ways in the dark night; but faith is the sun of righteousness. Shining the sun of faith, we go forward the way of mercy and complete our journey ever praising God in heart.

11 November

Come now, and let us reason together, says the LORD; though your sins are as scarlet, they shall be as white as snow; though they are red like crimson, they shall be like wool.

Isaiah 1: 18

Redemption of Sin

God has already taken away sins of humans. He views the world through Christ to find no sin remaining. Our sins, like scarlet as they were, have already been whitened like snow, by the red hot blood of Christ. We see that our sins were wiped away by Christ. Redemption is not a matter of the future but a fact established. The only need left over is to turn human heart to God-ward. Turning our faces God-ward through Christ, we know there is no trace of our sins in the eyes of God.

12 November

Good Master, what shall I do to inherit eternal life? And Jesus said to him, Why do you call Me good? None is good except One, God.

Luke 18: 18–19

Creation of Good

God is of the good, and not of the evil and the human. God is the God of good, whereas Devil is the evil of human beings. God saves the world by creating the human beings of good. On the contrary, Devil destroys the good by tempting and deepening the human evils. Salvation virtually means the creation of the good.

13 November

Well done, good and faithful servant. You have been faithful over a few things; I will make you ruler over many things. Enter into the joy of your Lord.

Matthew 25: 21

Heaven as Workplace

The Heavenly Nation is not a place of rest, but of work. Christ does not say "Enter You into the rest of the Lord" but "Enter You into the joy of the Lord." God's joy is the joy of helping and guiding persons. Christians come to the Nation of Christ and enter into this joy. The Heavenly Nation is the place where love is unceasingly practiced. We are working for the Nation of Love with the Father eternally. Nothing is so beautiful as a Christian's concept of the Heavenly Nation. It is not a place for a lazy person to go. It's a place for an active person to go. It's a place where work is needed with a greater responsibility.

14 November

The Son of man, coming in the clouds with great power and glory, shall send His angels and shall gather His elect from the four winds, from the end of the earth to the end of heaven.

Mark 13: 26–27

Christians Among Nations

England is not a Christian nation, but a few Christians exist in England. America is not a Christian country, but a few Christians exist among Americans. In the same token, the world will not become Christian nations after all, but a few Christians will arise from among the nations. God shall not elect every one of a nation to His servant. Most of people will remain of this world. Then, upon the last judgment of this world, God "shall gather all His elect" from all the nations. The earth and everything upon it will be reduced to ashes; but those who love God will remain for ever, "shining more and more to the perfect day" (*Proverbs 4: 18*).

15   November

Do not fear those who kill the body, but are not able to kill the soul. But rather fear Him who can destroy both soul and body in hell.

Matthew 10: 28

Be Brave

Be brave first. Say no when you should say no and say yes when you should say yes. Be not afraid of the face of humans, for humans are by no means stronger than God. And God will destroy them who intend to kill you. A strong humans is just a shadow to perish soon. So far you are afraid of humans, you are afraid of the ghosts. Those who do not speak of the evident truth being afraid of humans are coward. Know the last victor is Jesus Christ after all. His enemies such as scholars, power-holders, and riches are "the moles and the bats who hide into the clefts of the rocks, and into the tops of the ragged rocks, for fear of the LORD and for the glory of His majesty, when He arises to shake the earth terribly" (*Isaiah 2: 21*).

16 November

How you are fallen from the heavens, O shining star, son of the morning. How you are cut down to the ground, you who weakened the nations.

Isaiah 14: 12

Fall and Salvation

Human is a fallen creature; that is what the Bible plainly teaches. The so-called natural human is an unnatural being; an abnormal, not a normal human. How human fell is difficult to explain; not perhaps exactly as is told in the Book of Genesis; but in some way must human has fallen, and become a God-forsaken, self-centric being. By this fall human became a helpless creature, unable by one's own effort to become what human ought to become. Only by the sovereign grace of the Almighty can human become a child of God. And the Gospel is the pronouncement of such a grace; and so it meets the deepest need of human. We are saved only because "GOD WILLS that all men and women should be saved and come to the knowledge of the truth (Gospel)" (*1 Timothy 2: 4*).

17 November

God commends His love toward us, in that, while we were yet sinners, Christ died for us. Much more then, being now justified by His blood, we shall be saved from wrath through Him.

Romans 5: 8–9

Cornerstone of Love

Good deeds of a Christian come from the love of God. "While we were yet sinners, Christ died for us." I am encouraged to shun evil and do good, not as moral obligation, but simply by Christ's love. I can give good deed to the world when my heart is full and overflows of love. "Woe is to me, if I preach not the gospel" (*1 Corinthians 9: 16*). Woe, indeed, is to me, if I neglect following after good deeds. Overflowing love within my heart, I burst with joy. No one else could deprive it from me. I am really crazy with the love of Christ.

18 November

Turn to Me, and be saved, all the ends of the earth; for I am God, and there is no other. I have sworn by Myself, the word has gone out of My mouth in righteousness, and shall not return, that to Me every knee shall bow, every tongue shall swear.

Isaiah 45: 22–23

Faith and Experience

I trust in the Word of God, and not in my experience of salvation. My experience may be illusion, but the Word stands for ever. The Word says: "Turn to Me, and be saved." I turn to the Crossed One by faith, and I believe that I am saved. I will not be one of those who will not believe unless they see signs and wonders. The experience of salvation is not necessary for the assurance of salvation. The Cross is the assurance. Sins may remain, or may not; but I am not to turn to my sins, but to the Cross. The Cross does sanctify, that I believe; but I do not be sanctified in order to be assured of my salvation. Enough that Christ was crucified for me. The peace which passes all understanding is mine. And such a faith does sanctify me. Faith is first, and sanctification follows faith; not vice versa. To place sanctification before faith is Roman Catholicism, Americanism, and all other forms of legalistic religion; opposed to the spirit of Protestantism, and I believe, of Christian Religion.

19 November

You may know that the Son of man has power on earth to forgive sins (then says he to the sick of the palsy), Arise, and take up your bed, and go to your house. And he arose, and departed to his house.

Matthew 9: 6, 7

Forgiveness of Sins

God forgives sins. He does not merely promise to forgive; but does forgive in fact and deed. Subjectively, we know forgiveness through the removal of guilt from our conscience. Once forgiven by Him, sin remains no more in us, which pained our sense of guilt. Like a bite of poisonous snake before vaccine, sin is powerless before the forgiveness of God, although it retains its ugly form. "For sin shall not have dominion over you, for you are not under law, but under grace" (*Romans 6: 14*). Objectively, we know forgiveness of our sins by our ability to forgive sins of others. Our sins forgiven, we forgive sins of others. We all know, how difficult it is to forgive other's sins committed against us. We think we have already forgiven them; but the antipathy remains in us only to be revived by any slight provocation. It is only by having our sins forgiven by God, that we are enabled to completely forgive the sins committed against us. Human comes to forgive others since he or she is first forgiven by the Creator. When that comes to being, I know that I am saved and created as a child of God.

The sure sign that my sins are forgiven is that I can freely forgive the sins of others. Though my profession of Christianity be perfect in all other respect, I am still in sins and unsaved, not forgiven and saved by God if I could not forgive sins committed by others against me.

20 November

We joy in God through our Lord Jesus Christ, by whom we have now received the atonement.

Romans 5: 11

My Peace and Joy

My peace and joy are not in the success of my works, not in the ever new attainment of knowledge, and not in the satisfaction of my conscience, but in Christ and His Cross. By looking at the Cross and waiting upon Him, there are in me peace and joy that pass all understanding. They who think I am a man of works, they who think I am a man of thought, and they who treat me as a moralist, they know not the Redeemer who is at the foundation of my very being.

21 November

The love of God was revealed in us, because God sent His only begotten Son into the world that we might live through Him. In this is love, not that we loved God, but that He loved us.

1 John 4: 9–10

God Loves First

God first loved us; not we loved Him. First we are loved by God, and then we are enabled to love Him. Unlike the ruler of this world, God shows us his love without our offering of something praiseworthy. For God is our Father, and not an exploiter. We should not expect Father's gift by pressing a certain doctrine. Let Himself do that best rejoice Him. Let us stand before Him as His pure children. It is beyond our power to become a warrior of Christian faith. Even if this is possible, we shall not count it praiseworthy of faith. Let God fight on our behalf. We, Christians, should be proud of this highest and greatest gift.

22   November

Who then is Paul, and who is Apollos, but servants by whom you believed, even to each the Lord gave? I have planted, Apollos watered, but only God gave the increase.

1 Corinthians 3: 5–7

Seek God Directly

The Father who raised Jesus Christ from the dead saves each person directly, not through humans or institutions (*Galatians 1: 1*). Salvation is precious because God directly involves the salvation of each person. Thus it is grave misconception to seek salvation through a priest or a guru of humans, instead of God Himself. Each person is a child of God and therefore should go to the Father directly without medium of others. One will be disappointed to others to whom one asked what should be asked to God directly. The want of the soul is only fulfilled by God; it cannot be made up by any person even Paul, Peter, or the Pope. Human warship is a serious obstacle to pure faith. Rely on God alone and leave from the dependence on humans.

23 November

Behold, the LORD's hand is not shortened so that it cannot save, nor is His ear heavy so that it cannot hear. But your iniquities have come between you and your God, and your sins have hidden His face from you, from hearing.

Isaiah 59: 1–2

Moral Causes of Affliction

Affliction has to have its physical causes or moral reasons. To us, it is the failure to obey the voice of God, calling to repentance. Are we not hiding in our hearts anything offensive? Are we not clouding clear righteousness? Is there not a Cain among ourselves? (*Joshua 7: 1–26*) Are we not invoking God's anger on ourselves by pocketing unlawful wealth and possession? These are the questions we have to ask and answer ourselves whenever confronted with any trials. Happy is the human who discovers one's own sin each time and gets strokes of God's rod.

24 November

The gospel which was preached of me is not after human. For I neither received it of human, neither was I taught it, but by the revelation of Jesus Christ.

                              Galatians 1: 11–12

Influence and Spirit

Not influence, but the Spirit of God is essential. Influences are circumstances, atmospheres both material and moral, social surroundings, church-connections, and anything involved with one's own interest; they are of earth. But the Spirit is a will-power that works from within, revelatory, individualistic, and without one's own interest; it is of heaven. One's mind is truly converted not by influences, social or churchly, but by the all-powerful Spirit of God. Paul become an apostle, not by Jerusalemite or Antiochian influences, but by the will of God. Let us cease to speak of influences, as do pagans and materialists, but of the Spirit of God, as all true Christians ought to do.

25 November

The word of the LORD came to me, saying, Jeremiah, what do you see? And I said, I see a rod of an almond tree.

Jeremiah 1: 11

Prophet is Poet

A prophet is a poet, and a poet is a prophet. It is difficult to make distinction between them. One may say, "the prophet is a spokesperson of the will of God, while the poet is a speaker of the heart of the nature." But this distinction does not stand. For a poet cannot understand the heart of the nature without knowing the will of God, and a prophet cannot know the will of God without understanding the nature. Every prophet understands the nature, and every poet knows the will of God. Both the prophet and the poet are the messenger of God; they are directly called by God, not by humans or institutions. Both are the same type of person, who stands closest to living God; they are neither a priest who manipulates ritual magic nor a theologian who disputes letters.

26 November

The days of our years are 70 years; and if by strength they are 80 years, yet their fruit is labor and sorrow; for it is soon cut off, and we fly away.

Psalms 90: 10

Life is Perfect

Life is perfect for the purpose for which it is designed. It is perfect as a means for perfecting our personality, although life is imperfect as an end. "Tribulation works patience; patience, probation; and probation, hope" (*Romans 5: 3–4*). Life through its tribulations bring about the sure hope of glory. Life properly used is a perfection. Life is very transitory; the days of our years are 70 years, and their fruit is labor and sorrow. Yet life in its transitoriness prepares us for the bliss that fades not away. Knowing the meaning of life, no one like Job curses the day of his birth: "Let the day perish wherein I was born" (*Job 3: 3*).

27 November

You are My friends if you do whatever I command you.

John 15: 14

Jesus, Eternal Friend

People feel loneliness even surrounded by many friends. Some, however, are ever joyful and happy even without a friend. The one is a friend of eternal and always lives in loneliness. And Christ is the only friend of the person. With Christ as the friend, one can ever enjoy happiness even deprived of any friend on earth.

28   November

Come, blessed of My Father, inherit the Nation prepared for you from the foundation of the world. For I was hungry, and you gave Me food; I was thirsty, and you gave Me drink; I was a stranger, and you took Me in; I was naked, and you clothed Me; I was sick, and you visited Me; I was in prison, and you came to Me... Truly I say to you, Inasmuch as you did it to one of the least of these My brothers, you have done it to Me.

Matthew 25: 34–36, 40

Angel in Sickbed

I have not seen an angel of the heaven. But I saw my beloved angel in sickbed with her marble countenance, "bell-ring" voice and tears of morning dew. She must be an angel. Such a one, even if unable to rise from sickbed and stays by my side lifelong, will never be me grief. She is my daily consolation. Purifying and elevating me, she impresses me with the guardianship of an angel. Do you want to see an angel? Go and see a chaste lady in sickbed. She is an angel spiritually.

29 November

Before I formed you in the belly I knew you; and before you came forth out of the womb I consecrated you, and I predestined you a prophet to the nations.

Jeremiah 1: 5

Mission of Japan

Japan is a laboratory of Asia, as Greece was for Europe. The future of Asian is determined by Japan, as the history of Europe was by Greece. The character that Japan adopts and the religion, the philosophy and the arts that Japan develops will influence over the Asian and endure as their model. It will be compared to the Greek such as Solon, Phidias, and Plato, who founded the Western civilization. Thus we know the responsibility of Japan is not just for the welfare of millions of the fellow people, but for the future of trillions of people in the east of Himalaya. How heavy responsibility we have to bear.

30 November

O LORD, I know that the way of human does not belong to one's self; it is not in human who walks to direct one's own steps.

Jeremiah 10: 23

Our Way

The way of human is not in one's self. Human cannot direct one's own steps. He or she has to live beyond one's own will since he or she has neither wisdom nor power. What he or she dislikes he or she has to do. What he or she likes he or she has to give up. He or she is no commander of one's own destiny, but is a poor, wandering sheep. An inch adjacent can be searched out but miles ahead cannot be known. Oh God, pray, let us walk in meek to Your guidance.

01 December

Behold, I will do a new thing; now it shall spring forth; shall you not know it? I will even make a way in the wilderness, and rivers in the desert.

Isaiah 43: 19

Evolution and Bible

I believe that the Bible is true; I also believe that evolution or rather science is true. The Bible is true in the realm of spirit, and science is true in the realm of senses. The reconciliation of the Bible with science is as difficult as that of spirit with senses, of the Invisible with the Visible. Still I believe that the two is one at the bottom, perfectly reconcilable like the two lobes of the brain or the two arms of the body, one just as indispensable as the other. Is there not evolution in the Bible itself, and do we not observe special creation (called it "mutation," or by any other name may be) in the evolutionary processes of life, sudden unexplainable changes, apparently self-generated, but nevertheless fundamental and epoch-making. I observed such a change in my own life; I call it "Christian conversion," a sudden leap from one stage of life to another. So I am forced to be an evolutionist and a special fundamentalist at the same time. Both are the facts of life, and I cannot deny them.

02 December

And I said to you, You are My servant; I have chosen you, and not cast you away. Do not fear; for I am with you; be not dismayed; for I am your God. I will make you strong; yes, I will help you; yes, I will uphold you with the right hand of My righteousness.

Isaiah 41: 9–10

Secret of Success

Do things which you are compelled from outside, and you will succeed it unfailingly. If you do things that you want to do, it will fail inevitably. The compelled condition is not your manipulation, but God's dictation. The will of God is fulfilled and the desire of self is failed. The secret of success is to do things that God compels.

03   December

Now has been made plain, and by the prophetic Scriptures, according to the commandment of the everlasting God, made known to all nations for the obedience of faith.

Romans 16: 26

Endurance of Bible

Christianity renews itself year after year, while other religions die away in the process of history. The old Bible has not perished along with the times. Is this due to the perfectness of its philosophy? Unlikely. Rather, endurance of the Bible is due to the eternity of God, who quickens the human heart with His truth in all scenes. And as long as God abides, the truth of the Bible shall not lose its vitality. Believing in God, we shall embody the truth of Christianity and be partakers of its salvation.

04   December

The Nation of God is not in letter, but in power.

1 Corinthians 4: 20

Power of Christianity

God is not theory but power. Life is not logic but practice. Religion of salvation must be of a great power. Literatures cannot save human. Philosophy cannot transform the world. If Christianity is God's truth, it should not be merely to please humans like literature or philosophy. The word of God "converts the soul" (*Psalms 19: 7*). "It is quick and powerful, and sharper than any two-edged sword, piercing even to the dividing asunder of soul and spirit, and of the joints and marrow, and is a discerner of the thoughts and intents of the heart" (*Hebrews 4: 12*). "It is the power of God unto salvation to everyone that believes; to the Jew first, and also to the Gentile" (*Romans 1: 16*). Christianity did not come "with Excellency of speech or of wisdom" (*1 Corinthians 2: 1*).

05 December

The Nation of Heaven is like a grain of mustard seed, which a person took and sowed in one's field; which indeed is the least of all seeds, but when it is grown it is the greatest among herbs and becomes a tree, so that the birds of the air come and lodge in its branches.

> Matthew 13: 31–32

Everlasting Truth

Truth, like a grain of mustard seed, grows even to eternity. Salvation by Christ is truth. Luther heard this to stand up; Bunyan heard this to his rest. But, what made Luther the Luther was not merely the word of his master, Staubitz. Luther needed still his solitary thinking and prayer over 3–4 years at the monastery. Even the passionate Bunyan, after realizing the great truth of remission of sins, took 12 years, drilling at the Bedford Prison. To possess a great truth, whether of reason or of faith, is to make a great stride ahead. But any influence, however sensational or emotional, which does not touch upon our reason, will sooner or later be reduced to nothing.

06 December

I will ransom them from the power of the grave; I will redeem them from death. O Death, where are your plagues; O Grave, where is your ruin. Repentance shall be hidden from My eyes.

Hosea 13: 14

Things Not Be Afraid

The first that we should not be afraid of is failure. It is a guidance of God to alter the compass of life. After repeated failures we come to know the mission of life designated by God. The second that we should not be afraid of is tribulation. It is an occasion on which God drives us to the pasture of rest. He prepares it for us. The third that we should not be afraid of is death. It is the last operation to separate the pure gold of sanctified souls from the damned of flesh. Crossing death, we come to the Nation of Glory for the saints of God.

07 December

God said to Moses, I AM THAT I AM; and he said, Thus shall You say to the children of Israel, I AM has sent me to you.

Exodus 3: 14

God Is

God Is. How blessed thought it is! God the loving Father, who is love itself, "Is"; He exists, rules, and takes care of the world, mankind, my country, my home, and me. What more do I need? Everlasting peace should be mine, although the world is in turmoil, nations arming themselves to the teeth. The future is all unknown, dark and terrible, even though diplomats toil hard to bring about a universal peace; indeed darkness covers the earth, and the people, as was as foretold by a prophet (*Isaiah 60: 2*). But "God Is" settles the problems of the world. All is right. We can rest and sleep in peace, as Jesus the Son of God slept at the stern of the ship which carried His disciples over the furious waves of the sea (*Matthew 8: 23–27*).

08 December

Take heed to yourselves, lest your hearts are overcharged with entertainment, intoxication, and cares of this life, and so that day come upon you unawares. for it shall come as a snare on all those sitting on the face of the whole earth. Watch therefore, praying always that you may be counted worthy to be saved all these things which shall come, and to stand before the Son of man.

Luke 21: 34–36

Prophecy of Judgment

The true believers look up to Jesus not as the liberator of this world for social reform, home purification or moral edification, but as the savior at the great day of God's judgment. When Felix, the governor, came with his wife Drusilla, he sent for Paul, and heard him concerning the faith in Christ. And as Paul explained righteousness, temperance and judgment to come, Felix trembled, and answered, "Go your way for this time; when I have convenient season, I will call for you" (*Acts 24: 24–25*). And what lacks of the present day preachers, theologians, clergymen and missionaries is a warning about the coming judgment, which sufficed the governor to tremble.

09 December

One who believes on Me, as the Scripture has said, "Out of one's belly shall flow rivers of living water"

John 7: 38

Living Water

A person of faith works always. The person never gets tired because he or she does not dissipate one's own power. Practically, however, a power comes to and through a person, so that he or she can work by one's self. Is this not an ideal life? "Without haste and without rest," as Goethe's motto. But Christians are working daily more than what the poet dreamed of. A new power will be given, as we believe; and therewith we can do anything. Believing in Christ is leaving one's whole body and soul to His care. Thus a Christian will turn out to be a reservoir, flowing forth rivers of living water to quench many a thirsty soul.

10 December

In Jesus Christ we have redemption through his blood, the forgiveness of sins, according to the riches of his grace.

Ephesians 1: 7

Forgiven Sinner

Believers in Christ have, by faith, God's vitalities. Their spirits and actions should at least follow Christ, who is the Lord of the Heavenly Nation, of which the citizen is a little Christ. To put it another way, the citizens of the Heavenly Nation are sinners forgiven. They are never the persons of virtue, moralists, philanthropists, nor theologians. Neither are they millionaires nor peers. But they are the person who repented their sins, confessed before God, attained God's salvation, and transformed to a new creature. These are, in fact, the citizens of the Heavenly Nation in Christianity.

11 December

I have trodden the wine-press alone; and of the people there was none with me; for I will tread them in my anger, and trample them in my fury; and their blood shall be sprinkled upon my garments, and I will stain all my clothing.

Isaiah 63: 3

Friend of Heart

We are solitary but not isolated. We have many friends because we are solitary. What is solitary? It is to make one's heart a friend. One who makes one's heart a friend is the friend of every person who makes one's heart a friend. One who seeks friends in the social intercourse has merely limited number of friends at a party. But one who seeks a friend in one's heart is a friend of the universe. Every person who sorrows in the heart, pursues the ideal of the heart, serves God in the heart, and is saved by the Lord in the heart is our friend. True friendship is spiritual and of the heart.

12   December

Now you also put off all these; anger, wrath, malice, blasphemy, filthy communication out of your mouth. Lie not one to another, seeing that you have put off the old person with your deeds; And have put on the new person, which is renewed in knowledge after the image of Christ that created you;

Colossians 3: 8–10

Son of God

A person is not God's child by nature, but becomes God's child by the faith of Christ. One is corruptible by nature, but becomes incorruptible by the eternal life of Christ: "Because I live, you shall live also" (*John 14: 19*). Human is nothing; God is everything. Human is a precious being only because he or she can know of one's worthlessness and then can live with God.

13 December

I beseech you therefore, brothers, by the mercies of God to present your bodies a living sacrifice, holy, pleasing to God, which is your reasonable service.

Romans 12: 1

Everyday Christianity

The feast of Christians is their daily life. This is a feast that Christians worship God with a life of holy and righteous love, and not with rituals and offerings. Who can call Christianity a superstition? Who can please God by mere words of worship or by observances of complicated rituals, if the one ignore one's daily life? What God asks us is our everyday practice of love and righteousness. Look at Paul; his words turn rituals into ethical practice. He lived and taught religious and ethical life at the same time.

14   December

Be strong and of a good courage, fear not, nor be afraid of them; for the LORD is your God, He goes with you; He will not fail you, nor forsake you.

Deuteronomy 31: 6

Be a Hero

Be a hero. Say No when you must say No, and say Yes when you must say Yea. Be not afraid of the faces of humans. They can never be stronger than God; and if they attack you, God will crush them. The strongest of humans is a mere shadow, soon to pass away and no more. Be not afraid of ghosts of humans. Be not cowards when you speak plain truth before humans. Be specially a hero in confessing Jesus Christ before heathens and unbelievers. Know that after all Jesus is the Conqueror, and that His adversaries, be they religionists, statesmen or plutocrats, are like bats and moles hiding in the clefts of rocks "when He arises to shake terribly the earth" (*Isaiah 2: 21*).

15 December

Knowing this first, that no prophecy of the scripture is of any private interpretation. For the prophecy came not in old time by the will of human; but holy persons of God spoke as they were moved by the Holy Spirit.

2 Peter 1: 20–21

Book of God

The Bible is a book of God. God's nature, will, power, and mercy are most clearly and most faithfully written in the Bible. Some books may describe these issues; but none other than the Bible makes known God to us so vividly, as if looking up to the sun without a tint of ambiguity. The Bible starts with "God said" not with "Thus I heard." The Bible does not try to prove God's existence, but says "In the beginning was God." Not only has the Bible an intuitive style but, in revealing the truth, it manipulates nothing to reason or imagination. Nobody has seen God face to face; but the writers of the Scriptures were constantly inspired in mind with direct touch of God. Therefore, we rely on the Bible to know God.

16 December

The Spirit helps our infirmities. For we do not know what we should pray for as we ought, but the Spirit Himself makes intercession for us with groanings which cannot be uttered. And He searching the hearts knows what is the mind of the Spirit, because He makes intercession for the saints according to the will of God.

Romans 8: 26–27

Essence of Prayer

I do not pray myself, but let the Spirit pray for me. The Spirit, dwelling within me, pray through me the will of God, often with groanings that cannot be uttered. This is my true prayer. Philosophically incomprehensible but experimentally true, the Spirit prays to God through and in His children. It is my prayer because I let the Spirit do it for me. This prayer is acceptable in the sight of God and is sure to be heard precisely because its contents are not my wishes and desires but His holy will. Thus renunciation of self is necessary for prayer even when addressing God for help. We must pray that God may pray for us.

17 December

In returning and rest shall you be saved; in quietness and in confidence shall be your strength.

Isaiah 30: 15

Trust Lord Quietly

Rely on God and wait His instruction and salvation quietly and at rest. You will then get strength, be stronger, be able to conquer your foes, and be saved. When arrows of enmity fall into me, when whole nations oppress me, when I stand alone like a lamb among wolves, I have simply to keep quiet, hope all deliverance by God. Let Him be my strong tower of defense, my guard and my weapon. I am weak, but He is strong. With Him, I am stronger than the whole world. Salvation rests with Jehovah. Pray, Father, Your mercy be upon Your people.

18 December

The Father has made us meet to be partakers of the inheritance of the saints in light; He has delivered us from the power of darkness, and has turned us into the Nation of his dear Son; In whom we have redemption through his blood, the forgiveness of sins.

Colossians 1: 12–14

My Experiment

Forgiveness of sin is not my thought of meditation, not my doctrine of belief, and not my creed of confession, but my experiment. It is the cause of my salvation and the cornerstone of my faith. Without it, my faith is in vain and I am still in the bondage of sin. I am saved not by my good deeds, not by my repentance, and even not by my faith, but by the abolishment of sin which God achieved through Christ. Salvation is not on my side at all; it is altogether on the other side. Salvation does not depend on my psychic state, but it is the achievement of Christ, who died for me when I was still in the midst of sin. Salvation has been already achieved by Christ for me when I did not know. I just realized Christ's salvation and entered into it.

19   December

Our Father, who is in Heaven,
hallowed be Your name.
Your nation come,
Your will be done, as in Heaven,
so also on the earth.
Give us day by day our daily bread,
and forgive us our sins
so that we also forgive everyone
who commits sin to us.
And lead us not into temptation,
but deliver us from evil.

Luke 11: 2–4

Prayer is Poetry

Our prayer is not prayer in general. We do not pray for what we need. God is Father of Love and gives us all that we need, without our appeal, without waiting for our prayer. Prayer means spontaneous overflowing of our innermost heat. It is verbal expression of our sense of gratitude which cannot be held silent. Or it means tears crystallized out of sorrow which cannot be bound. This may be called poetry, if not called a prayer. A Christian prayer may well be defined to be poetry singing in the presence of God.

20 December

I live by the faith of the Son of God, who loved me, and gave himself for me. I do not set aside the grace of God; for if righteousness come by the law, then Christ is dead in vain.

Galatians 2: 21

Mystery of Faith

Some believers grieve their inadequate faith, but they do not understand what Christian faith is. Faith is not any self-power such as solid conviction or force of believing. It is reliance and dependence upon someone apart from one's self. Look up to His righteousness, His holiness, His salvation and then receive them one's own. We should not possess our own faith, or better to have none at all. Poor, naked, and powerless as we are, we can still wish to live with Him alone, without lamenting our least faith. We would rather rejoice having none of our own faith. Without our own, we are driven to depend; and by depending we catch the true faith. Let there be no more grievance about insufficient faith, upon realizing this mystery of faith.

21 December

Whom have I in Heaven? And besides You I desire none on earth. My flesh and my heart fail; but God is the strength of my heart, and my part forever.

Psalms 73: 25–26

With God

Sweet is to be alone with God. Nothing to give out but to receive. Nothing to give up but to be granted. I feel then wholly joy in the depth of mercy, absorbing it through every-one of my prose. I would then take and say the words of Peter at the mount of transfiguration, "Lord, it is good for us to be here" *(Matthew 17: 4)*. The Lord will not leave us for long. He will send us to the world to witness what blessings we have received. We shall then suffer pain and sorrow from the world. We are thus compelled by the Lord to hold relationship with the world. Never do we, from our own interest, seek social relationship.

22   December

As Moses lifted up the serpent in the wilderness, even so must the Son of man be lifted up; That whosoever believes in him should not perish, but have eternal life.

John 3: 14–15

If No Christ

What if Christ did not come into this world? Say not that we have Confucius, Lao-tzu, Buddha, Muhammad, Plato, Alexander, Caesar. What if then we have had no Christ? I might have played a hero, willing to give life in the battlefield; I might have acted a bandit to assassinate the people's enemy; or I might have been a philanthropist gladly offering my body for the sake of the forsaken. But the thank to Christ for sins forgiven, we shall inherit the heavenly blessings: the joy of being counted a child of God, the joy of dying to myself and living in God, the hope of resurrection, and the promised land of eternal life.

23   December

My soul shall be satisfied as with marrow and fatness; and my mouth shall praise You with joyful lips, when I remember You on my bed and think of You in the night watches. Because You have been my help, therefore in the shadow of Your wings I will rejoice.

Psalms 63: 5–7

Faith and Theology

Faith is poem, song, and music. It is neither meditation nor doctrine. Faith is just what "I believe." It cannot know how to explain itself. Faith is the voice of life within. So, it sings itself and dances from within, as found in Paul. His expression, unlike those of modern times, belongs to a type of poetry, and not a result of systematic thinking. Luther says, "Theology is a type of music." True theology, thus, can be found only where perfect harmony, boundless joy, union with the universe and life exist and where reason and spirit, hand in hand, dance and rejoice together. A Christian, then, is a thinker as well as a poet according to one's faith and perception. He or she views all creatures in harmony, setting one's self in the standpoint of Jesus Christ, the only begotten son of God: "by Christ all things consist" (*Colossians 1: 17*).

24 December

The Lord Himself shall descend from heaven with a shout, with the voice of the archangel and with the trumpet of God. And the dead in Christ shall rise first. Then we who are alive and remain shall be caught up together with them in the clouds, to meet the Lord in the air. And so we shall ever be with the Lord.

1 Thessalonians 4: 16–17

Christmas in Heaven

Christmas reminds me of many friends who have passed away to live with the Lord. We may celebrate Christmas with sorrow because they are not with us on the earth. Our beloved ones, who joined our joyful Christmas, are no longer to be seen among us. This renders our merry Christmas rather depressed. But then the words of Paul come, "brethren, sorrow not, even as others which have no hope," and appeal the more strongly to our mind. A lonely Christmas without our beloved ones will not last long. "So also will God, through Jesus, bring back those who sleep, together with Him" (*1 Thessalonians 4: 14*). What a great consolation! We are assured of reunion with them to joy true Christmas in Heaven. This must be true Christmas.

25   December

The angel said to them, Fear not; for, behold, I bring you good news of great joy, which shall be to all people. For to you is born this day in the city of David a Savior, which is Christ the Lord. And this shall be a sign to you; You shall find the babe wrapped in swaddling clothes, lying in a manger. And suddenly there was with the angel a multitude of the heavenly host praising God, and saying, Glory to God in the highest, on earth peace, and joy toward humans.

Luke 2: 10–14

Joy to World

A voice of joy came out of a newly born baby. Its chorus shakes the whole house with gladness. A new Man came to us with hope. The heavens shook with joy when, in Bethlehem at evening, the Son of Man gave His first voice. The Last Adam came forth to humanity, bringing eternity. Heavens, then, echoed with the earth, singing "A Baby Son of Man was born among humans." All creatures, then, sang in a voice "Our emancipation has come." Christmas is a holy day for the universe; a day for the celebration of liberation, freedom and perfection of heavens, and the earth and everything in them.

26 December

Now the birth of Jesus Christ was on this wise; When as his mother Mary was espoused to Joseph, before they came together, she was found with child of the Holy Spirit. Then Joseph her husband, being a just man, and not willing to make her a public example, was minded to put her away privily. But while he thought on these things, behold, the angel of the Lord appeared to him in a dream, saying, Joseph, you son of David, fear not to take to you Mary as your wife; for that which is conceived in her is of the Holy Spirit.

Matthew 1: 18–21

Virgin Birth of Christ

The Virgin Birth of Christ is certainly a miracle, and it is not to be explained by science and ordinary experiences. But it is only one of the many miracles which constitute the bases of Christian beliefs. The Resurrection (*1 Corinthians 15*) is a miracle, the Ascension (*Acts 1: 9*) is a miracle, and the Second Advent (*1 Thessalonians 4: 13–18*), the Last Judgment, the Consummation of All Things (*Matthew 25: 31–46*), are all to be miracles. Miracle-less Christianity is not Christianity at all. God dwelling among persons, divinity entering into humanity, the heaven coming down to save and renew the earth; this is what we celebrate on Christmas. We celebrate an amazing miracle on Christmas, and wait and hope for other miracles which shall bring our redemption to completion. Glory to God in the highest.

27 December

No one has greater love than the person who lay down one's life for one's friends.

John 15: 13

Christ and Friendship

Christ is the center and core of friendship. Apart from Him, there is no true, deep, enduring friendship. What He said is very true: "He that gathers not with Me scatters" (*Luke 11: 23*). Friends that gather not with Him must scatter, sooner or later. So it was that when Christ was born in Bethlehem, true friendship came into this world. So angels sang on the Holy Night: "Glory to God in the highest, And on earth, peace among men and women" (*Luke 2: 14*); that is, friendship, neighborliness, and enduring fellowship among them.

28   December

Though Christ was rich, yet for your sakes he became poor, that you might be rich through his poverty.

2 Corinthians 8: 9

Wealth in Poverty

Poverty means a life of sincerity. Faith comes out of sincerity. Love and hope come out of sincerity. Poverty is exemplified by the earthly life of the Lord Jesus. We best understand Jesus in our poverty. True wealth means being with Jesus. A Christian does not pursue after any wealth other than this.

29   December

These all died in faith, not having received the promises, but having seen them afar off. And they were persuaded of them and embraced them and confessed that they were strangers and pilgrims on the earth. For they who say such things declare plainly that they seek a fatherland. And truly, if they had been mindful of that country from which they came out, they might have had opportunity to have returned. But now they stretch forth to a better fatherland, that is, a heavenly one. Therefore God is not ashamed to be called their God, for He has prepared a city for them.

Hebrews 11: 13–16

Home in Heaven

With the advance of faith, this world will be non-sense, and the world to come will gain ever increasing meaning. My body yet remains here like looking the star though the curtain but my heart is already transferred there to the glory. The more I am longing there, the lighter I will be here. Confidence in there which is already prepared for us, we can perceive our worldly desires diminishing day by day. Then, our hearts flow out of joy, hearing the heavenly music and seeing the glory. All trials will be ended; all tears will be wiped away in this world; Jesus will welcome us face to face;

We will reunite with our beloved; all puzzles will be solved; all misunderstandings will be reconciled; and we will enter a new life of unbounded liberty. A this-worldly persons complain that life is short. But a Christian never complain the shortness of one's life, for the homeland of heaven lies now before our eyes.

30 December

Paul, an apostle, not of men, neither by man, but by Jesus Christ, and God the Father.

Galatians 1: 1

By Will of God

"Paul, an apostle by the will of God," (*1 Corinthians 1: 1*) not by his own choice, not by his resolution, and not by his speculative study of Christian truth, but solely by the will of God, by His sovereign grace, by His election, "foreordained before the foundation of the world" (*1 Peter 1: 20*). So is every Christian "born, not of blood, nor of the will of man, but of God" (*John 1: 13*). He is not "Christianized" by missionaries, but is pressed by the all conquering, all-compelling will of God into His Nation and its service. Oh, the sovereign will of God, stronger than my will, than my sin even. Nothing else made me a Christian; nothing else keeps me in the faith; nothing else will save me at last. "Thanks be to God for His unspeakable gift" (*2 Corinthians 9: 15*).

31 December

Give thanks to the LORD, call on His name, make known His deeds among the people. Sing to Him, sing psalms to Him, talk of all His wondrous works. Glory in His holy name, let the heart of those who seek the LORD rejoice.

1 Chronicles 16: 8–10

End of Year

This year is leaving, and another year is coming. Thank God for many a good thing of this year, and for evils likewise. Thank God for each and every thing. God's will was done; His glory was raised. My life is not for me, but for God and for fulfilling His will. God is my Lord and I am His servant. A servant is happy and satisfied with sacrificing oneself, only to see Lord's work well done. God advances His work year-in and year-out unceasingly. This year has also seen a progress of the accomplishment of His will with magnified glory. Here is my thanksgiving, beyond the questions of my sufferings or losses. More so, when I recall the many blessings granted upon me.

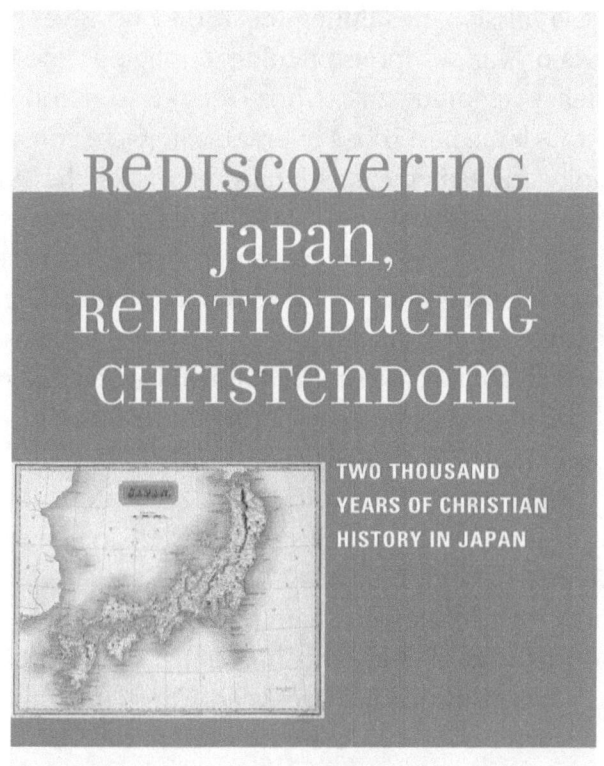

Rediscovering Japan Reintroducing Christendom: Two Thousand Years if Christian History in Japan (Samuel Lee)

In *Rediscovering Japan, Reintroducing Christendom* Japan's unvoiced Christian history and cultural roots are examined from an alternative perspective. It is commonly believed that Christianity was introduced to Japan by the Spanish and

Portuguese missionaries during the 1500s; however, Samuel Lee draws on various forms of cultural, religious and linguistic evidence to argue that Christianity was introduced to Japan through the Lost Tribes of Israel, who were converted to Christianity through the missionary efforts of the Assyrian Church of the East around A.D. 500. Much of the evidence he discusses has become submerged into many Japanese folkloric songs, festivals and is to be found in temples. There are, for example, approximately 300 words in Japanese and Hebrew/Aramaic that are similar. Further, Dr. Lee outlines the history of Catholicism in Japan during the 1500s, the systematic persecution of Christians from 1600s to the 1800s, and the rise of Protestant Church in Japan. The historical portion of the book ends with an analysis and discussion of 21st century Japanese society. Lastly, in *Rediscovering Japan, Reintroducing Christendom,* Samuel Lee questions the missiological methods of Western Christianity and advocates an approach based in dialogue between Christianity and other cultures. For ore information about the book visit http://web.me.com/slwe/Rediscovering_Japan/the_Book.html or check the book at amazon.com

Reviews

"undoubtedly one of the best books available on the 2000 years of Christian history in Japan."

— **Arimasa Kubo, President, Remnant Publishing & Lecturer on Biblical Japan Forum**

"A unique and challenging view of the historic overlap between Japanese Shintoism and Buddhism and Christianity. It is a pleasure to observe the depth of his awareness."

— **Prof. Toshifumi Uemura, Japan Lutheran College**

"[Lee's] research, which has become an enormous source book in the history of Japanese Christianity, culture and language suggests that it is indeed possible that the Japanese people originated from Israel..."

— **Hiroko Ayabe, founder of Japan Revival Ministries, Tama Gospel Center**

"Lee offers a truly unique point of view and necessary commentary on the subject of Christian mission in today's world. This work is to be highly recommended."

— **Brian McLaren, author,**
Church on the Other Side* and *Everything Must Change: Jesus, Global Crisis & a Revolution of Hope

"One of the most exciting and provocative contributions to discussions of global Christianity that I have read in a long time A fascinating, in-depth and detailed portrait His argument is compelling and extremely well-documented..."

— **Carl Raschke, Professor of Religious Studies, University of Denver, author,**
The Next Reformation and GloboChrist

PUBLISHER
Hamilton Book / Rowman & Littlefield Publishing Group
ISBN 0-7618-4949-1 / 978-0-7618-4949-0
www.hamilton-books.com
Price 29.95US$

UNDERSTANDING JAPAN
Through the Eyes of Christian Faith
Third Edition
SAMUEL LEE, PhD

Understanding Japan Through the Eyes of Christian Faith, Third Edition (Samuel Lee)

Understanding Japan through the Eyes of Christian Faith. is a fascinating book, combining Sociology and Christian worldview in a systematic manner and simple language. Samuel Lee has skillfully examined various facets of the Japanese society and culture looking for answers of why Christianity is not widely accepted and practiced in Japan. After dealing the historical background of Christianity in Japan and describing the socio-cultural condition of the nation, the author comes up with strategies and suggestions of how Christianity should approach Japan and suggests that Christianity should be reintroduced in Japan. Understanding Japan through the Eyes of Christian Faith. is a sociological and spiritual handbook for missionaries, mission organizations, churches, Christian Universities/Colleges and every Christian who is interested in reaching Japan. Japan is now ready to embrace the Gospel. You can discover it by reading this book.

PUBLISHER
Foundation University Press
www.foundationuniversitypress.com
ISBN 978-9490179014 Price 14.95US$

www.ingramcontent.com/pod-product-compliance
Lightning Source LLC
Chambersburg PA
CBHW020633230426
43665CB00008B/159